FIRST 50 SONGS

YOU SHOULD PLAY ON DOBRO®

Arranged by Fred Sokolow

Editorial assistance by Ronny S. Schiff

ISBN 978-1-5400-6745-6

HAL•LEONARD®

Visit Hal Leonard Online at
www.halleonard.com

Contact us:
Hal Leonard
7777 West Bluemound Road
Milwaukee, WI 53213
Email: info@halleonard.com

In Europe, contact:
Hal Leonard Europe Limited
42 Wigmore Street
Marylebone, London, W1U 2RN
Email: info@halleonardeurope.com

In Australia, contact:
Hal Leonard Australia Pty. Ltd.
4 Lentara Court
Cheltenham, Victoria, 3192 Australia
Email: info@halleonard.com.au

CONTENTS

ABOUT THE AUTHOR

Fred Sokolow is best known as the author of over 200 instructional and transcription books and videos for guitar, banjo, Dobro®, mandolin, lap steel, and ukulele. Fred has long been a well-known West Coast, multi-string performer and recording artist, particularly on the acoustic music scene. The diverse musical genres covered in his books and videos, along with several bluegrass, jazz, and rock CDs he has released, demonstrate his mastery of many musical styles. Whether he's playing Delta bottleneck blues, bluegrass or old-time banjo, '30s swing guitar, or screaming rock solos, he does it with authenticity and passion.

Fred's other books that may be of interest:

- *Fretboard Roadmaps for Dobro®,* book/online audio, Hal Leonard LLC.

- *Fretboard Roadmaps for Slide Guitar,* book/online audio, Hal Leonard LLC.

- *Fretboard Roadmaps for Lap Steel,* book/online audio, Hal Leonard LLC.

Email Fred with any questions about this or his other instruction books or DVDs at: Sokolowmusic.com.

INTRODUCTION

Played with a slide and lap-style, the Dobro® is an essential part of bluegrass, Hawaiian music, country music, early Western swing and, sometimes, blues. This book is a collection of the most popular, Dobro-associated tunes of all these genres, plus some rock/pop tunes that lend themselves to slide playing.

Because Dobro players tune the instrument various ways for different effects, several tunings are used in the 50 arrangements presented here. Bluegrass players tune to an open G chord (from the sixth string to the first string, GBDGBD); open D tuning is often used for blues (DADF♯AD); and C6 (CEGACE) is often used in Hawaiian music, Western Swing, and early country/western.

Dobro is short for "Dopyera brothers," the team that began manufacturing resonator guitars in 1928. (Some Dobros are played upright, like non-resonator guitars, but the term "Dobro" is usually associated with lap guitars that are played with a slide.)

The resonator is a metal cone on the sounding board that makes the guitar louder, almost like an electric guitar. However, "Dobro" has become a generic term for similar resonator guitars made by many different companies. To further confuse the issue, the Dobro has also been dubbed lap guitar, steel guitar, Hawaiian guitar, hound dog guitar, resonator guitar, slide guitar...and more. Some of these monikers are also applied to the lap steel, which is simply an electrified, solid-body version of the Dobro. In the 1950s, the lap steel evolved into the pedal steel, an essential part of country music...but the wooden Dobro with a metal resonator, played lap-style, is still heard in contemporary music of many genres.

Most of the songs presented in this collection are an essential part of a Dobro player's repertoire. Some of them (especially some classic blues and pop/rock tunes) are included for fun because they sit well on a Dobro and because their original recordings included a slide guitar. Learning these arrangements will acquaint you with many of the licks,

techniques, and clichés of Dobro playing. By all means, listen to each song or instrumental via YouTube, iTunes, Amazon, Google Play, Bandcamp, or whatever platform you use to access music, before you try to read the music — it makes learning the tune so much easier! If you want some general instruction on Dobro playing, check out the book (with online audio), *Fretboard Roadmaps for Dobro®*, by this author, published by Hal Leonard LLC.

Enjoy learning these solos,

Fred Sokolow

P.S.: More often than not, the Dobro is an ensemble instrument, usually accompanied by a guitar or some other chording instrument. However, some of the following arrangements stand on their own since they include strums or thumb/bass-style fingerpicking that make accompaniment unnecessary.

P.P.S.: The lyrics written under the tab/music are there to help you correlate the solos to the songs. Normally, one wouldn't sing while playing solos. Additional lyrics are also presented so you can perform these songs in their entirety, in addition to playing the solos.

Aloha 'Oe

Words and Music by Queen Liliuokalani

"Aloha 'Oe" ("Farewell to Thee") was composed by the Hawaiian queen Lili'uokalani circa 1877. It's one of Hawai'i's most famous songs. This arrangement includes the introductory verse, and Hawaiian and English lyrics.

C tuning:
(low to high) C-E-G-A-C-E

Key of G
Verse
Slow

Chorus

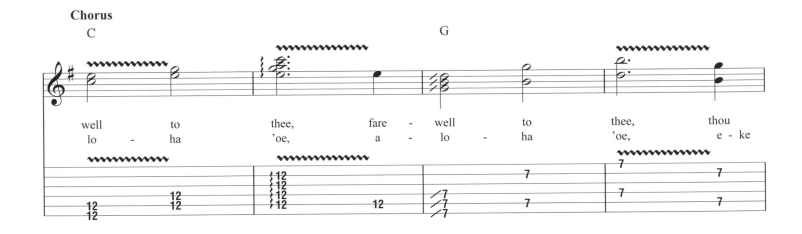

well — to — thee, fare — well to — thee, thou
lo — ha 'oe, a — lo — ha 'oe, e — ke

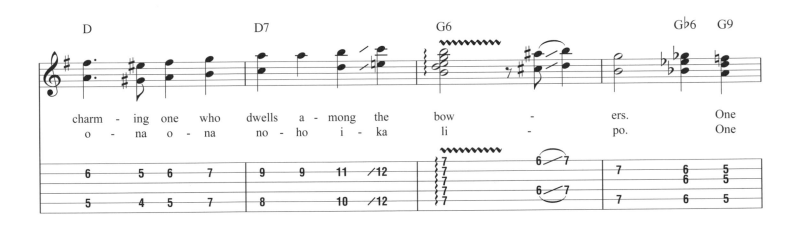

charm — ing one who dwells a — mong the bow — ers. One
o — na o — na no — ho i — ka li — po. One

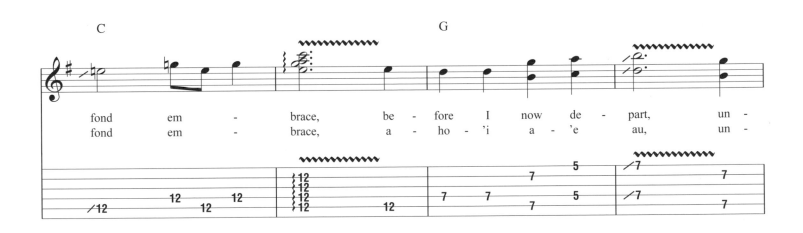

fond em — brace, be — fore I now de — part, un —
fond em — brace, a — ho — 'i a — 'e au, un —

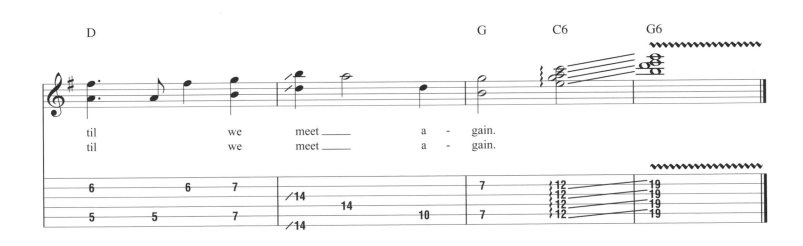

til we meet ____ a — gain.
til we meet ____ a — gain.

Amazing Grace

Words by John Newton
Traditional American Melody

John Newton, naval serviceman/slave trader/poet/evangelical cleric, wrote the words to this famous hymn in 1772. The melody was added in 1835 when composer William Walker adapted the melody of a shape-note song, "New Britain," to Newton's lyrics. Various legends surrounding Newton have inspired several movies, and the song is perhaps the most popular English language gospel tune of all time. In this arrangement, the second verse is played an octave lower than the first, with melody notes on the bass strings. *Play the down-stemmed notes with your thumb, the up-stemmed notes with your fingers.*

D tuning:
(low to high) D-A-D-F#-A-D

Key of D

Verse

grace that _____ taught my eyes to see, and ____

3. See additional lyrics

grace my _____ fears re - lieved. How ____

won - d'rous ___ did that ___ grace ap - pear, the ____

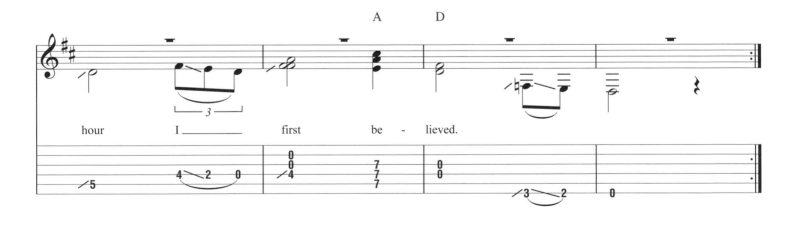

hour I _____ first be - lieved.

Additional Lyrics

3. When we've been there ten thousand years, bright shining as the sun;
   We'll have no less days to sing God's praise than when we first begun.

Beyond the Reef

Words and Music by Jack Pitman

Written in Hawai'i in 1948 by Canadian, Jack Pitman, "Beyond the Reef" is a popular "hapa-haole" tune—a song written in the Tin Pan Alley (early 20th century pop music) tradition, combined with the Hawaiian musical style. Hapa-haole songs are a hybrid mixture of western and Hawaiian influence.

The earliest hapa-haole favorites go back as far as 1903. Notice how the C6 tuning makes it possible to play the minor chords in this arrangement.

C6 tuning:
(low to high) C-E-G-A-C-E

Key of F

Blackberry Blossom

Traditional

It may have come from Ireland, but American fiddler Arthur Smith brought this fiddle tune to the attention of country and old-time music fans in the 1930s. Then, in the early 1960s, Bill Keith's banjo version made it a bluegrass standard—the pretty melody is a good showcase for Keith's innovative "melodic picking" style. It has become an essential bluegrass instrumental.

Like most fiddle tunes in the bluegrass repertoire, it is nearly always played in a certain key—in this case, the key of G. Also, like most fiddle tunes, it has an AABB structure: a four- or eight-bar phrase (A) is repeated, then a different four- or eight-bar phrase (B) is repeated. After playing AABB, you've gone once around the tune. That four-bar Intro is a typical fiddle-tune device sometimes called "potatoes," as in: "Start this tune with four potatoes." This arrangement goes around the tune twice, once with the melody on the lower strings, then in a higher register.

G tuning:
(low to high) G-B-D-G-B-D

Key of G

Intro

Brightly

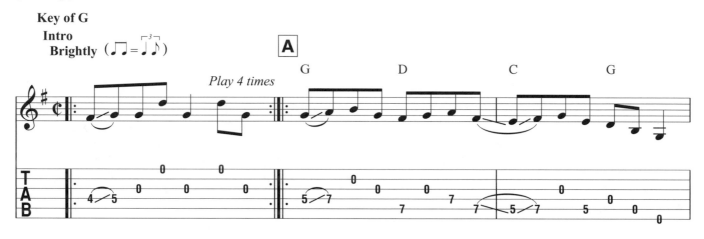

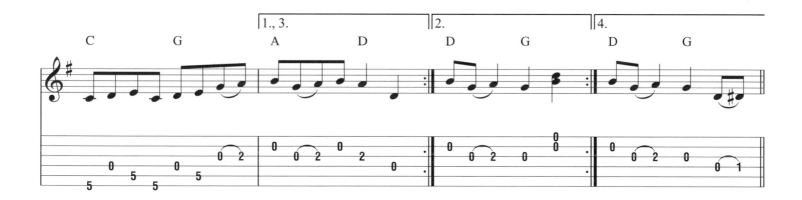

Blue Hawaii

from the Paramount Picture WAIKIKI WEDDING
Words and Music by Leo Robin and Ralph Rainger

Most people associate this tune with Elvis Presley's 1961 film, *Blue Hawaii*, but it was written in 1937 for *Waikiki Wedding*, a Bing Crosby movie.

C6 tuning:
(low to high) C-E-G-A-C-E

Key of G
Verse
Slow

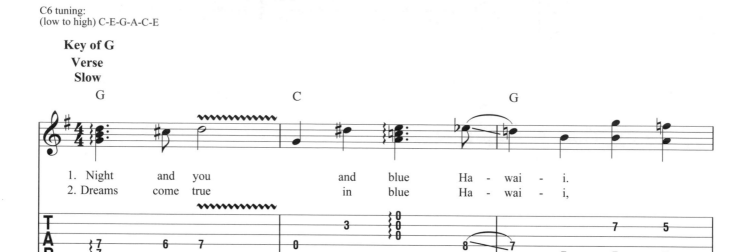

1. Night and you and blue Ha - wai - i.
2. Dreams come true in blue Ha - wai - i,

To Coda

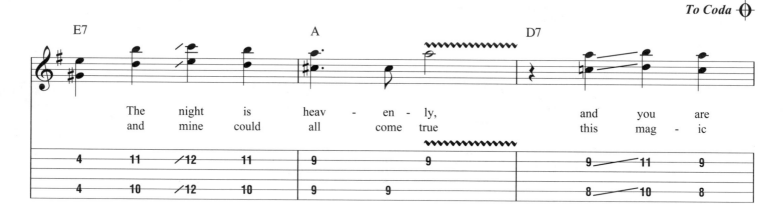

The night is heav - en - ly, and you are
and mine could all come true this mag - ic

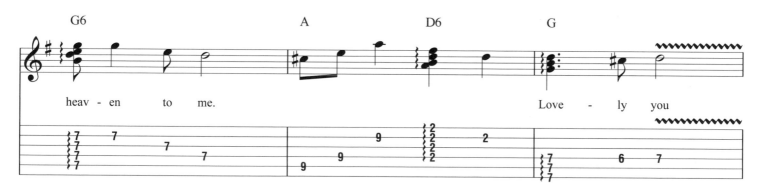

heav - en to me. Love - ly you

and blue Ha - wai - i. With all this

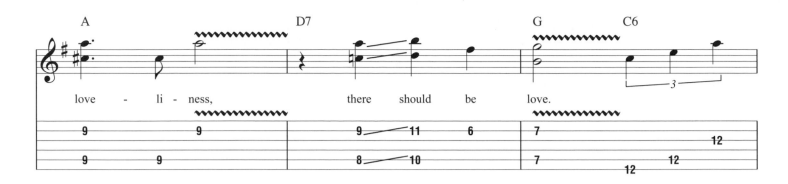

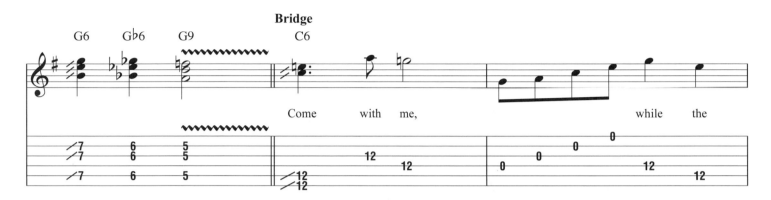

Bridge

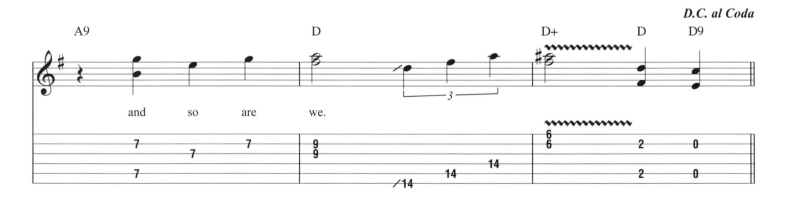

D.C. al Coda

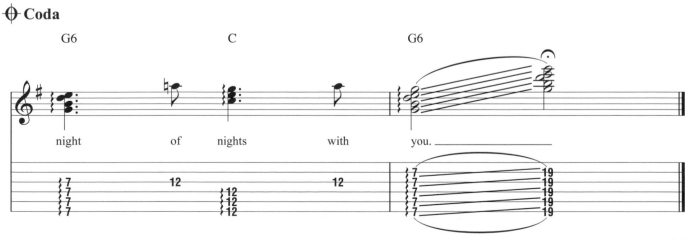

Coda

Blues Stay Away from Me

Words and Music by Alton Delmore, Rabon Delmore, Wayne Raney and Henry Glover

One of many famous "brother groups" of 1930s and '40s country music, the Delmore Brothers gave us "Deep River Blues," "Brown's Ferry Blues," "Gonna Lay Down My Old Guitar," "Freight Train Boogie," and many more classics. However, their biggest hit was 1949's "Blues Stay Away from Me." The song was bluesy enough to be covered by early rockers Gene Vincent, Johnny Burnette and the Rock 'n Roll Trio, and the Everly Brothers.

C6 tuning:
(low to high) C-E-G-A-C-E

Additional Lyrics

2. Love was never meant for me.
   True love was never meant for me.
   Seems somehow, we never can agree.

3. Life is full of misery.
   Dreams are like a memory,
   Bringing back your love that used to be.

4. Tears, so many I can't see.
   Years don't mean a thing to me.
   Time goes by and still I can't be free.

The Bottle Let Me Down

Words and Music by Merle Haggard

Merle Haggard, one of country music's greatest stars, wrote this song and scored a Top 10 hit on the country charts in 1963. That's when drinking songs in country music were about drowning one's sorrows…rather than partying. The solo in this arrangement has echoes of the iconic licks played on Haggard's recording by American rock and country guitar hero, James Burton.

G tuning:
(low to high) G-B-D-G-B-D

Key of D

drink e - nough to keep you off __ my mind.

Chorus

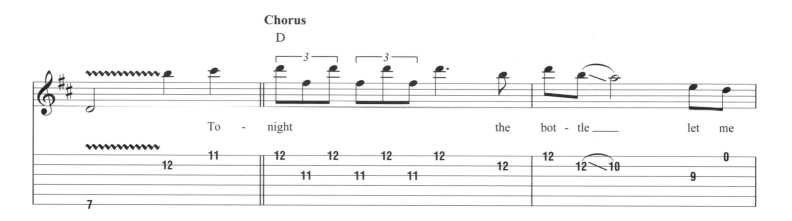

To - night the bot - tle __ let me

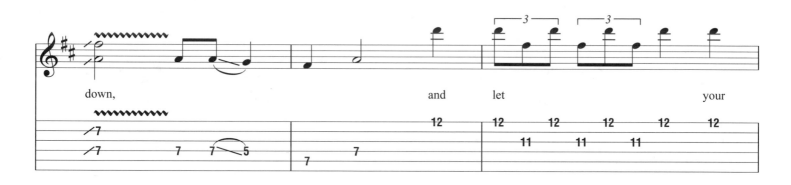

down, and let your

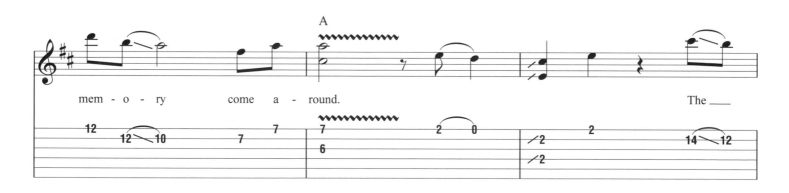

mem - o - ry come a - round. The __

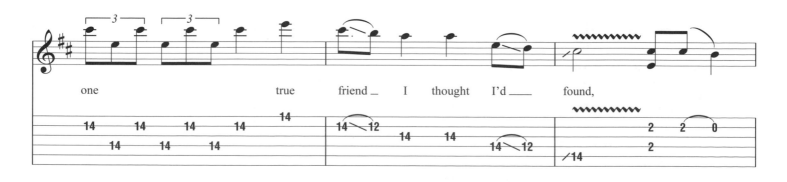

one true friend __ I thought I'd __ found,

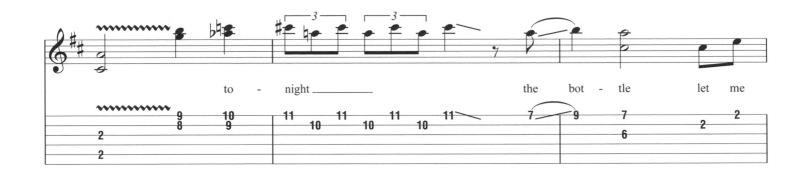

to - night _____ the bot - tle let me

To Coda ⊕

down.

Solo

D.S. al Coda ⊕ **Coda**

2. I've

Additional Lyrics

2. I've always had a bottle I could turn to,
   And lately I've been turnin' every day.
   But the wine don't take effect the way it used to,
   And I'm hurtin' in an old familiar way.

Can the Circle Be Unbroken
(Will the Circle Be Unbroken)
Words and Music by A.P. Carter

In 1935, the Carter Family recorded "Can the Circle Be Unbroken," a revised version of a 1907 hymn ("Will the Circle Be Unbroken") in which the singer describes his or her mother's funeral and declares that we'll all be reunited in heaven. The Carter family arrangement has become extremely popular and is often sung as a finale to a country music or bluegrass concert. Numerous singers and bands of all genres have recorded the tune.

The verse and chorus share the same melody. In this arrangement, the verse is played in first position and the chorus is played "up the neck."

G tuning:
(low to high) G-B-D-G-B-D

Key of G

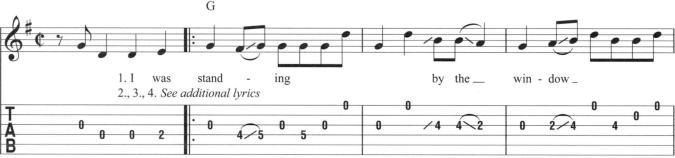

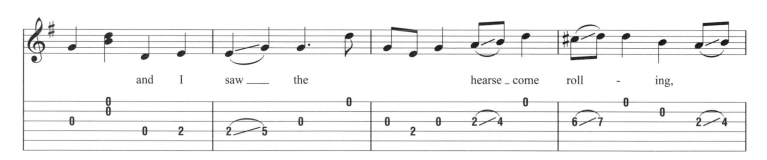

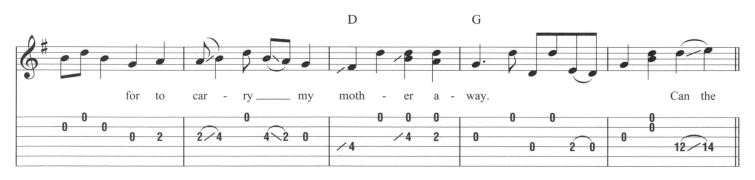

Chorus

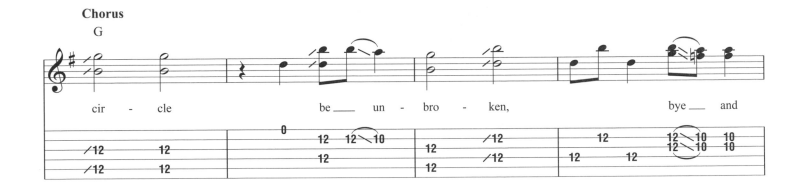

cir - cle   be __ un - bro - ken,   bye __ and

bye,   Lord, _   bye   and __   bye?   There's _ a

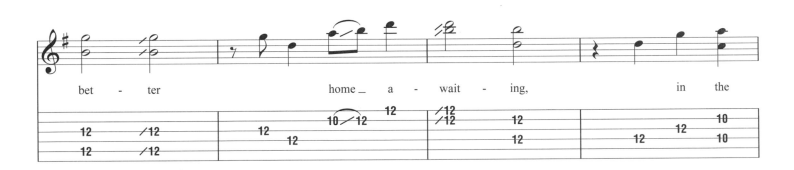

bet - ter   home _ a - wait - ing,   in   the

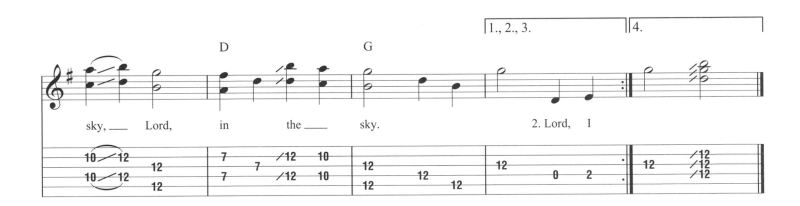

sky, __   Lord,   in   the __   sky.   2. Lord,   I

Additional Lyrics

2. Lord, I told the undertaker, "Undertaker, please drive slow,
   For this body you are hauling, Lord, I hate to see her go."

3. I followed close behind her, tried to hold up and be brave.
   But I could not hide my sorrow when they laid her in the grave.

4. Went back home, Lord, my home was lonesome, since my mother, she was gone.
   All my brothers, sisters cryin', what a home so sad and 'lone.

Cripple Creek

American Fiddle Tune

There's a Cripple Creek in Virginia and one in Colorado, and this key-of-A fiddle tune could refer to either one. The melody is well over a century old and words were put to it in the early 1900s, but bluegrassers play it as an instrumental. Popularized by Earl Scruggs, it's one of the first solos most bluegrass banjoists learn. Some Dobro players would capo up two frets and use G licks to play this tune, but this arrangement shows how to play it in A without a capo. The second B part is played an octave higher than the first.

G tuning:
(low to high) G-B-D-G-B-D

Key of A

Folsom Prison Blues

Words and Music by John R. Cash

Inspired by Gordon Jenkins' "Crescent City Blues," which shares many of the same lyrics and melody as "Folsom Prison Blues," Johnny Cash wrote the tune in 1955 on an airplane after seeing a movie about a convict at Folsom Prison. His Sun Records single reached #4 on the charts, but Cash's live version, recorded at Folsom Prison in 1968, went to #1 and became one of his signature songs.

The Intro and the solo that follows the vocals imitate the iconic licks played by Johnny Cash's lead guitarist, Luther Perkins.

G tuning:
(low to high) G-B-D-G-B-D

Key of G

Intro
Brightly

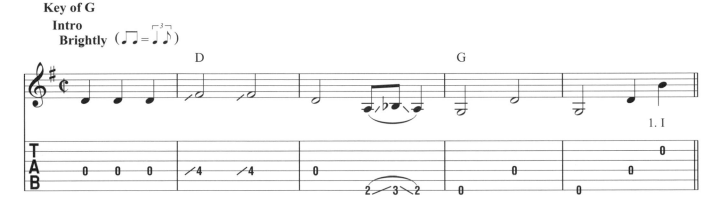

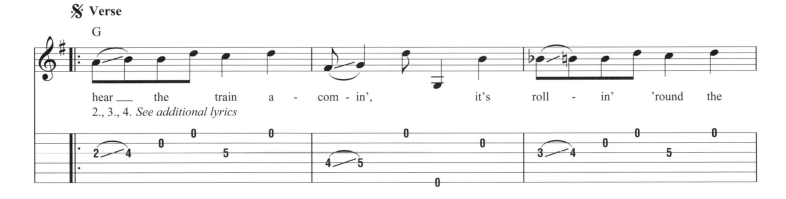

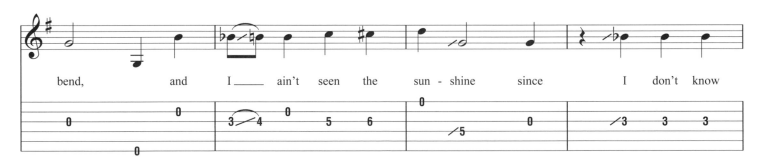

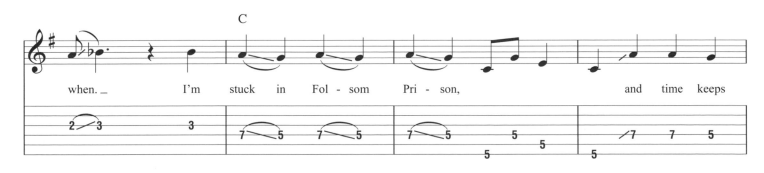

drag - gin' on.

But that train keeps a - roll - in' on down to

1., 3.

To Coda ⊕

2.

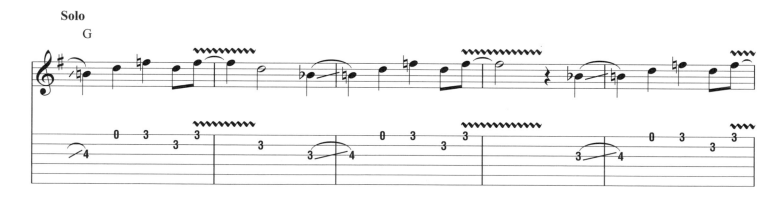

San ___ An - tone.

2. When
4. If they

Solo

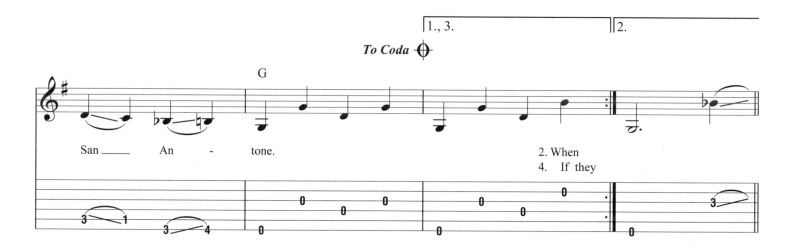

C

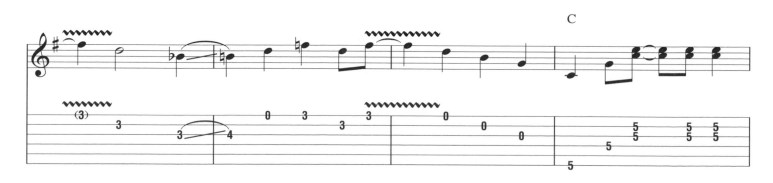

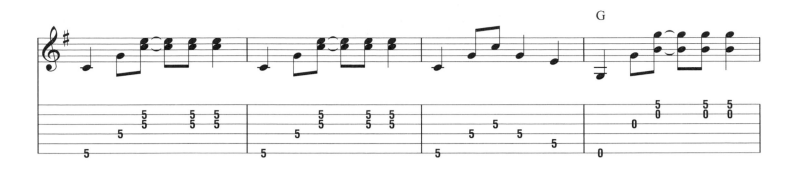

D.S. al Coda
(take repeat)

⊕ **Coda**

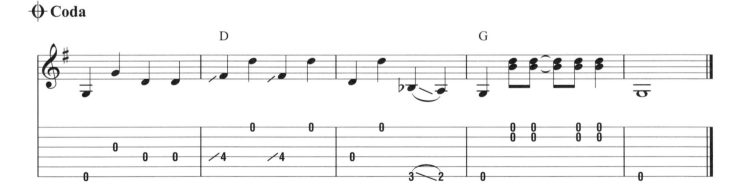

Additional Lyrics

2. When I was just a baby, my mama told me, "Son,
   Always be a good boy, don't ever play with guns."
   But I shot a man in Reno, just to watch him die.
   When I hear that whistle blowin', I hang my head and cry.

3. I bet there's rich folks eatin' in a fancy dining car.
   They're prob'ly drinkin' coffee and smokin' big cigars.
   But I know I had it comin', I know I can't be free.
   But those people keep a-movin', and that's what tortures me.

4. If they freed me from this prison, if that railroad train was mine,
   I bet I'd move it on a little farther down the line,
   Far from Folsom Prison, that's where I want to stay.
   And I'd let that lonesome whistle blow my blues away.

Death Letter Blues

Words and Music by Eddie "Son" House

Many 1930s-era acoustic blues guitarists recorded variations of "Death Letter Blues," a dire story of a man hearing the woman he loves has died…and there are many modern electric versions as well, most notably The White Stripes' radical interpretation. But Son House's 1960s performance of his version, with his National slide guitar, is the most powerful rendition by far. There are several videos (viewable on YouTube) of Son House playing his signature tune, and they are a testimony to how passionate and moving no-nonsense blues can be. It's a three-chord, twelve-bar blues with an often-repeated riff that is played between the vocal phrases. This arrangement includes an accompaniment to the vocal, reminiscent of Son House's playing, as well as a solo.

G tuning:
(low to high) G-B-D-G-B-D

Additional Lyrics

2. Well, I grabbed up my suitcase, I took off down the road.
   When I got there, she was laying on the cooling board.
   I grabbed up my suitcase, I took off down the road.
   When I got there, she was laying on the cooling board.

3. Well, I walked up right close, looked down in her face.
   Good old gal, you got to lay here 'til Judgment Day.
   I walked up right close, and I looked down in her face.
   Yes, been a good old gal, you got to lay here 'til Judgment Day.

4. Looked like ten thousand people standin' 'round the buryin' ground.
   I didn't know I loved her 'til they let her down.
   Looked like ten thousand, standin' 'round the buryin' ground.
   You know, I didn't know that I loved her 'til they let her down.

5. Well, I folded up my arms, I slowly walked away.
   I said, "Farewell, honey, I'll see you Judgment Day."
   Well, I folded up my arms, I slowly walked away.
   I said, "Farewell, honey, I'll see you Judgment Day."

6. You know I didn't feel so bad, 'til the good old sun went down.
   I didn't have a soul to throw my arms around.
   I didn't feel so bad, until the good old sun went down.
   I didn't have a soul to throw my arms around.

Dust My Broom

Words and Music by Elmore James and Robert Johnson

Elmore James's rendition of the Delta classic "Dust My Broom" was his signature tune—his band used to travel in a black and white Pontiac station wagon* with a big, yellow straw broom painted on it and a sign that read, "The Broomdusters." It was his first recording, made for Trumpet Records in 1952, with Sonny Boy Williamson accompanying him on harmonica. The original version went to #9 on the R&B charts. James re-recorded the song many times. One of the most recorded blues songs, "Dust My Broom" has been covered by ZZ Top, Homesick James, Albert King, Canned Heat, Fleetwood Mac, Ike and Tina Turner, and many more.

This arrangement includes a solo similar to the one James played (he used D tuning when playing slide guitar), and another solo that mimics the vocal line.

"Station wagons" were the precursors of today's SUVs.

D tuning:
(low to high) D-A-D-F#-A-D

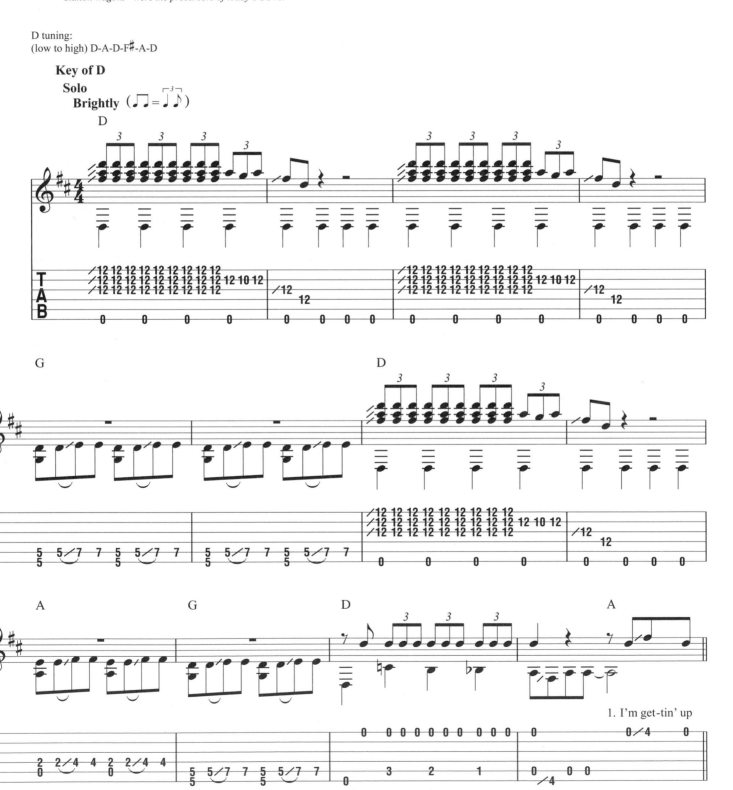

Verse

Additional Lyrics

2. I'm gonna write a letter, telephone every town I know.
   I'm gonna write a letter, telephone every town I know.
   If I don't find her in Mississippi, she's over in West Memphis I know.

3. And I don't want no woman want every downtown man she meets.
   No, I don't want no woman want every downtown man she meets.
   Man, she's a no-good doney, they shouldn't allow her on the street.

4. I believe, I believe my time ain't long.
   I believe, I believe my time ain't long.
   I'm gonna leave my baby and break up my happy home.

Faded Love

Words and Music by Bob Wills and Johnnie Lee Wills

Bob Wills, the great king of western swing, co-wrote "Faded Love" with his father, and his 1950 recording of the tune was a Top Ten country hit. Legendary guitarist, Eldon Shamblin, and fiddler/electric mandolin player, Johnny Gimble, were on that recording. Other artists who have scored Top Ten hits with the song include: Patsy Cline, Linda Ronstadt, Kenny Rogers (who took it to #1), and Willie Nelson.

The triplet figures in this arrangement are typical Dobro "fills." Played this way, triplets are a stylized way of sustaining a melody note.

G tuning:
(low to high) G-B-D-G-B-D

Key of G

Verse

Slow

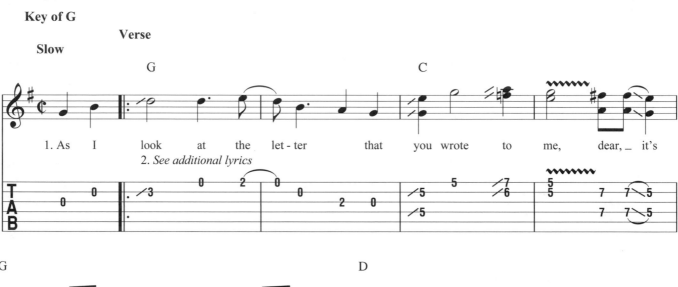

1. As I look at the let-ter that you wrote to me, dear, it's
2. *See additional lyrics*

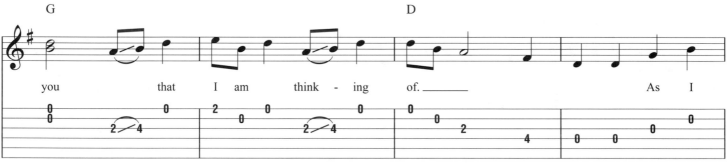

you that I am think-ing of. As I

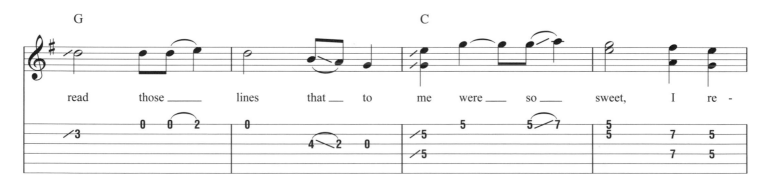

read those lines that to me were so sweet, I re-

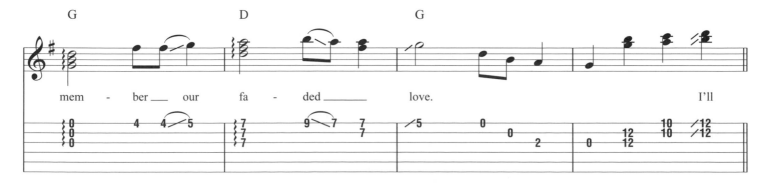

mem-ber our fa-ded love. I'll

Chorus

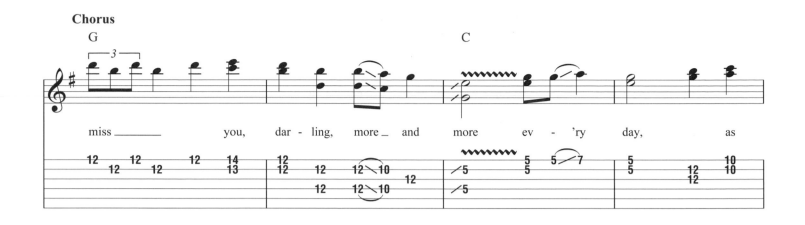

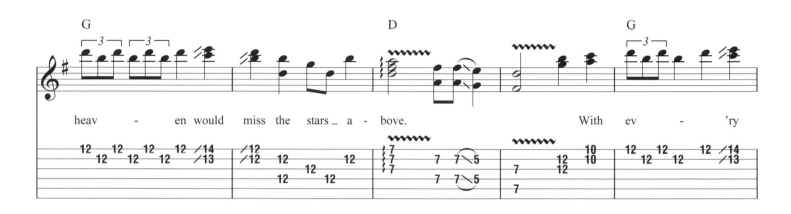

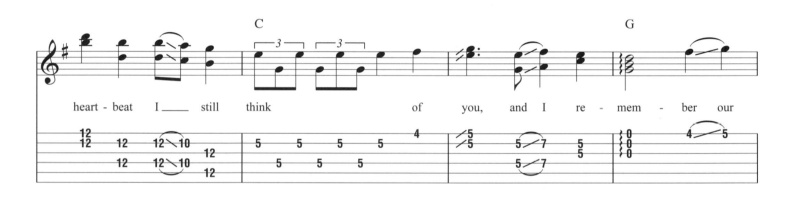

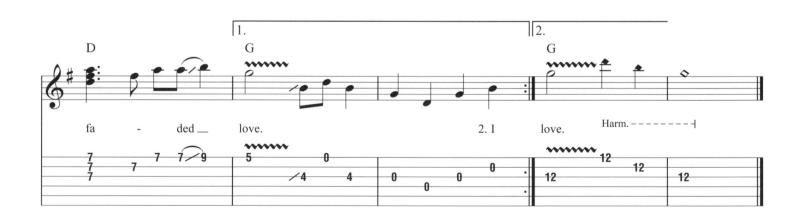

Additional Lyrics

2. I think of the past and all the pleasures we had as I watch the mating of the doves.
It was in the springtime that you said goodbye and I remember our faded love.

Fireball Mail

Words and Music by Fred Rose

One of many train songs in country music, "Fireball Mail" was a number one hit for Roy Acuff, the singer/songwriter/music publisher/Grand Ol' Opry star. His sideman Pete Kirby, known to the public as Bashful Brother Oswald, was one of the great Dobro players of country music. This arrangement shows how to play the tune in two different registers and includes many typical bluegrass licks and rolls.

G tuning:
(low to high) G-B-D-G-B-D

Key of G

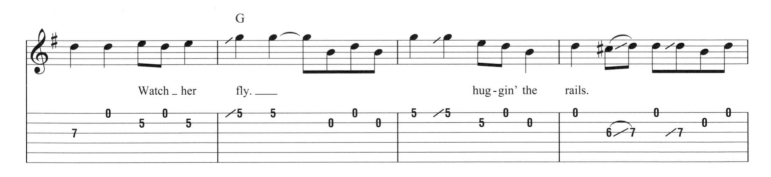

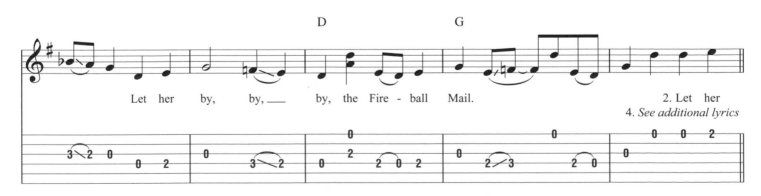

Verse

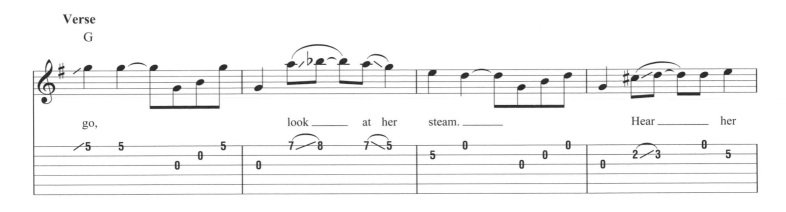

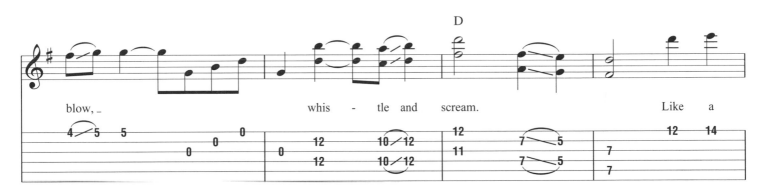

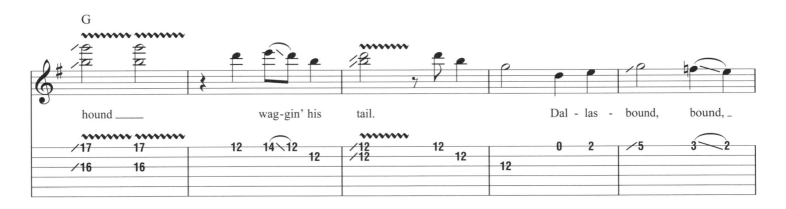

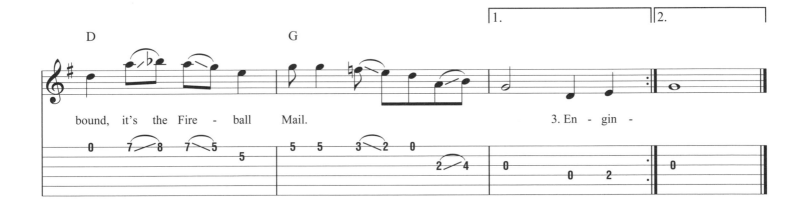

Additional Lyrics

3. Engineer makin' up time. Tracks are clear, look at her climb.
   See that freight clearin' the rail? Bet she's late, late, late; it's the Fireball Mail.

4. Watch her swerve, look at her sway. Get that curve out of the way!
   Watch her fly, look at her sail. Let her by, by, by; it's the Fireball Mail.

Foggy Mountain Rock

Words and Music by Louise Certain, Burkett Graves and Gladys Stacey

Josh Graves, also known as Buck Graves (and, when performing with Flatt and Scruggs and the Foggy Mountain Boys, "Uncle Josh"), was the premier Dobro player of bluegrass. His recordings with Flatt and Scruggs defined the role of the Dobro in that genre, just as Earl Scruggs's banjo playing defined the role of the banjo. The twelve-bar blues "Foggy Mountain Rock" is credited to Graves along with "Stacey and Certain," the pseudonyms for Flatt and Scruggs—Stacey and Certain were their wives' maiden names.

G tuning:
(low to high) G-B-D-G-B-D

Key of G

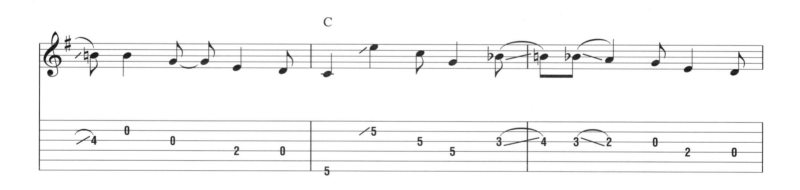

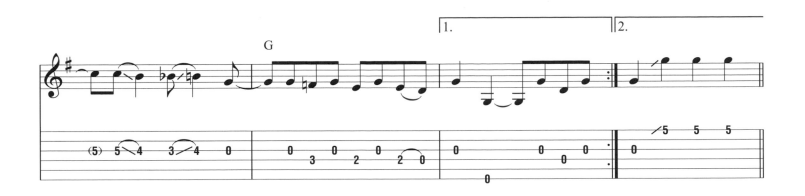

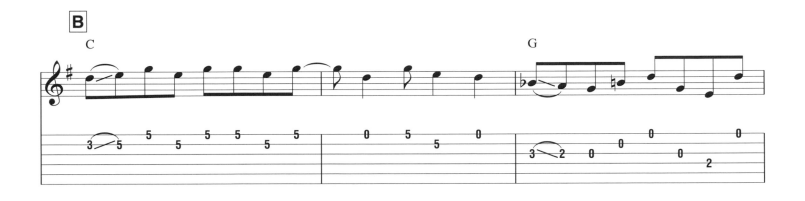

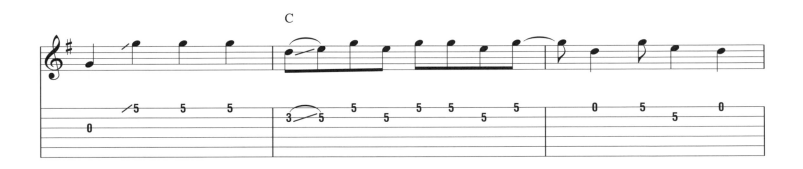

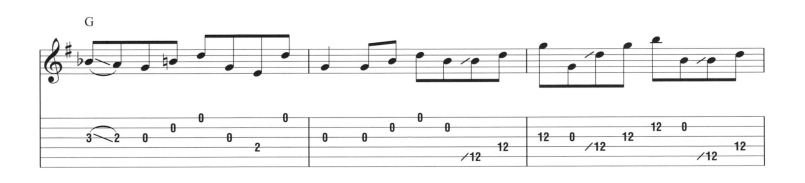

Free Bird

Words and Music by Allen Collins and Ronnie Van Zant

Lynyrd Skynyrd's 1973 hit, "Free Bird," is so iconic that it is inevitably requested at concerts (regardless of who is performing), both seriously and, sometimes, as a joke. It's usually played to end Lynyrd Skynyrd concerts and becomes a fifteen-minute jam.

In this arrangement, the second half of the verse is played an octave higher than the first half, to illustrate the two possible ways of rendering the melody.

G tuning:
(low to high) G-B-D-G-B-D

Key of G
Verse
Slow Rock Ballad

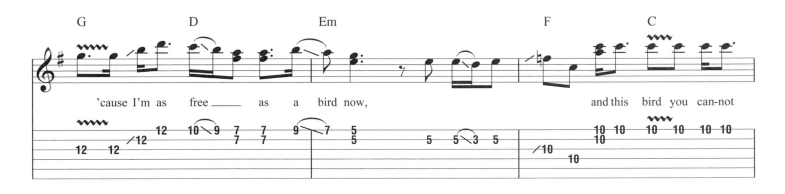

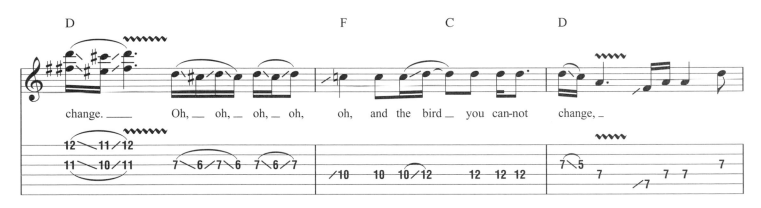

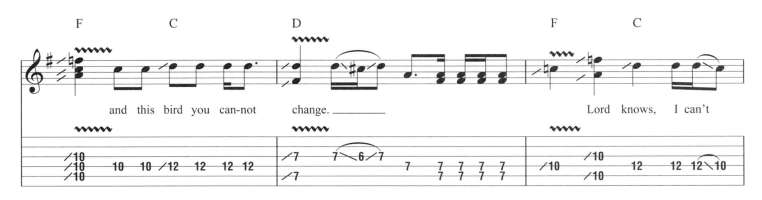

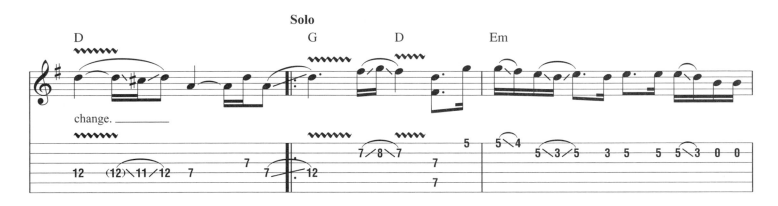

Greensleeves

Sixteenth Century Traditional English

This English ballad goes all the way back to the 1500s, and is also a popular Christmas song ("What Child Is This?") when sung with a different set of lyrics. Shakespeare mentioned the original song in his *The Merry Wives of Windsor*. It was said to be John F. Kennedy's favorite song. This arrangement demonstrates several ways to play pairs of notes that indicate a minor chord while in G tuning.

G tuning:
(low to high) G-B-D-G-B-D

Key of Dm

Verse

Moderately

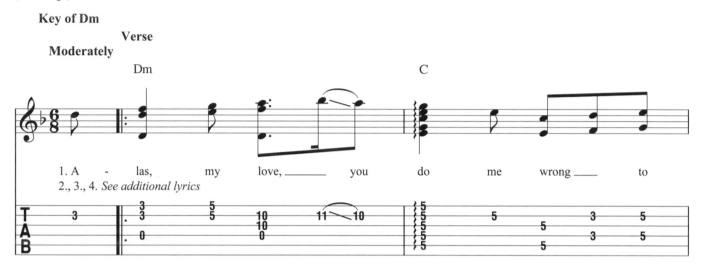

1. A - las, my love, _____ you do me wrong _____ to
2., 3., 4. *See additional lyrics*

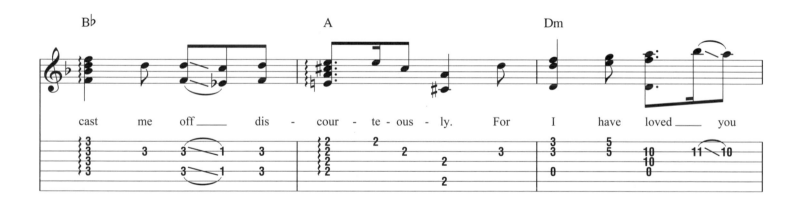

cast me off _____ dis - cour - te - ous - ly. For I have loved _____ you

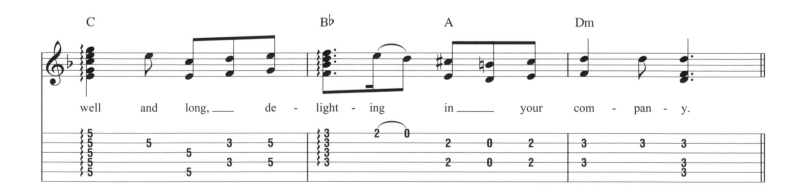

well and long, _____ de - light - ing in _____ your com - pan - y.

Chorus

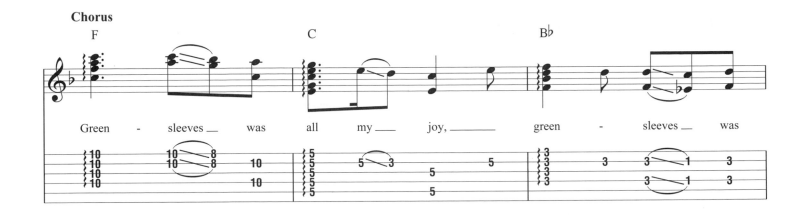

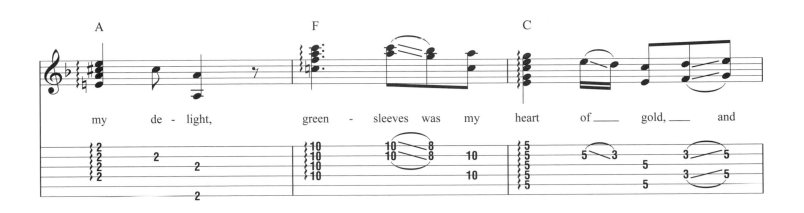

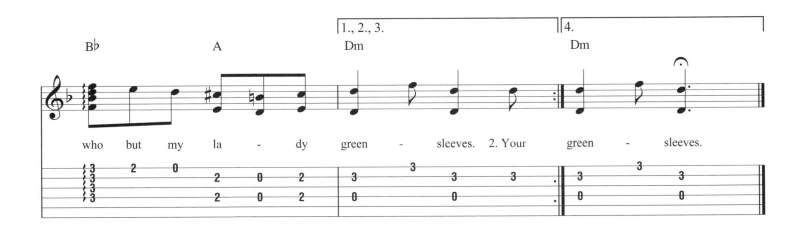

Additional Lyrics

2. Your vows you've broken, like my heart, oh, why did you so enrapture me?
   Now I remain in a world apart, but my heart remains in captivity.

3. I have been ready at your hand, to grant whatever you would crave.
   I have both wagered life and land, your love and goodwill for to have.

4. If you intend thus to disdain, it does the more enrapture me,
   And even so, I still remain a lover in captivity.

I Am a Man of Constant Sorrow

Words and Music by Carter Stanley

"I Am a Man of Constant Sorrow" was published in a songbook in 1913, and Bob Dylan included it in his first (1962) LP. The Stanley Brothers' 1959 recording was the template for the version in the 2000 film, *O Brother, Where Art Thou?*, which became a million-selling hit. In this very bluesy arrangement, the first half of the verse is played in first position with plenty of open strings; the second half is played in a higher register.

G tuning:
(low to high) G-B-D-G-B-D

Key of G

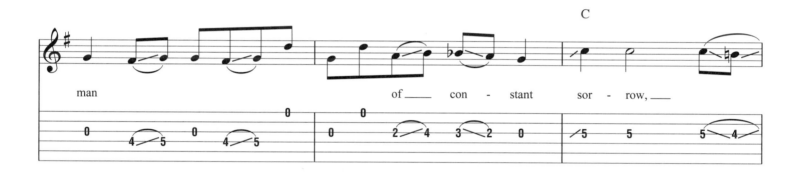

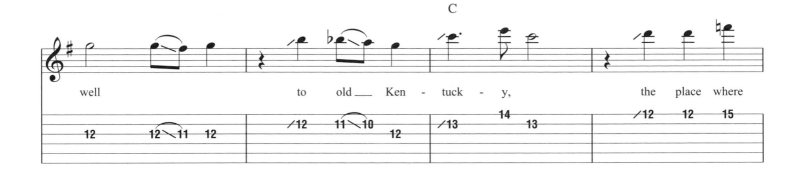

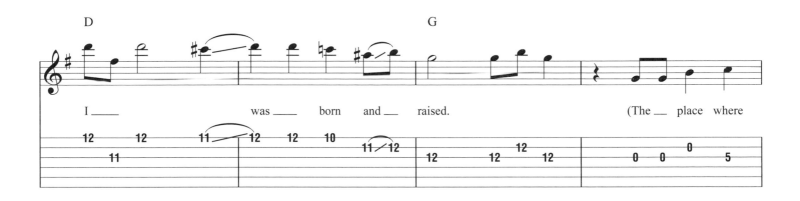

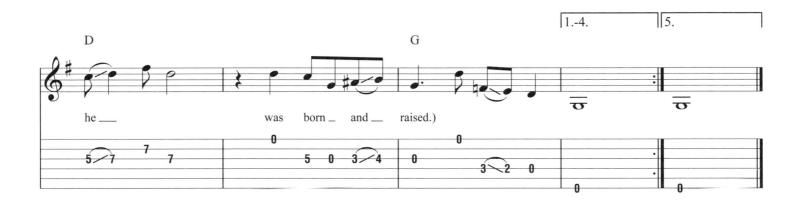

Additional Lyrics

2. For six long years I've been in trouble, no pleasure here on earth I find.
   For in this world I'm bound to ramble. I have no friends to help me now.
   (He has no friends to help him now.)

3. It's fare thee well, my own true lover. I never expect to see you again.
   For I'm bound to ride that northern railroad. Perhaps I'll die upon this train.
   (Perhaps he'll die upon this train.)

4. You can bury me in some deep valley, for many years where I may lay.
   Then you may learn to love another, while I am sleeping in my grave.
   (While he is sleeping in his grave.)

5. Maybe your friends think I'm just a stranger, my face you never will see no more.
   But there is one promise that is given: I'll meet you on God's golden shore.
   (He'll meet you on God's golden shore.)

I Can't Be Satisfied

Words and Music by McKinley Morganfield

The great Mississippi-born bluesman, Muddy Waters, wrote this tune and recorded it in 1948 for Chess Records in Chicago. The Rolling Stones, whose name came from a Muddy Waters song, included "I Can't Be Satisfied" on one of their early albums. Waters played the tune bottleneck-style, in open G tuning.

Waters' playing on the 1948 "I Can't Be Satisfied" is an example of an old-school, 1920s- and early 1930-style in which the song's melody is played and sung simultaneously, rather than playing a simple accompaniment while singing.

G tuning:
(low to high) G-B-D-G-B-D

Key of G

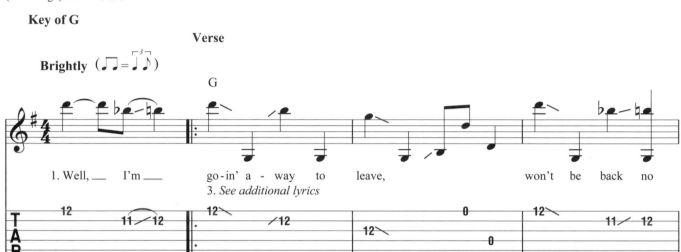

1. Well, ___ I'm ___ go-in' a - way to leave, won't be back no
3. *See additional lyrics*

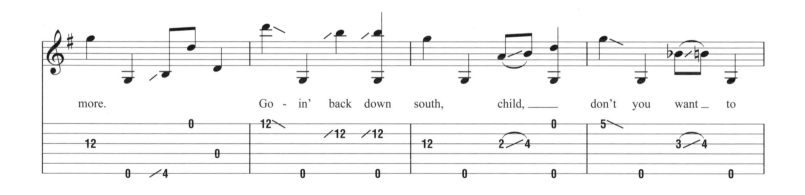

more. Go - in' back down south, child, ___ don't you want __ to

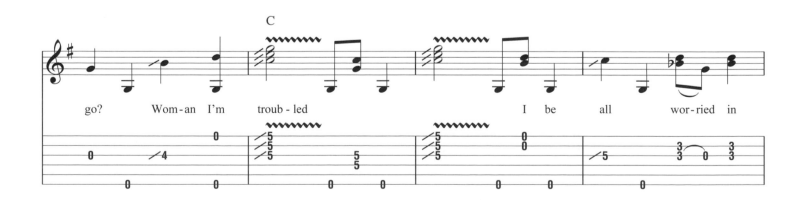

go? Wom-an I'm troub - led I be all wor-ried in

mind.   Well, babe, I

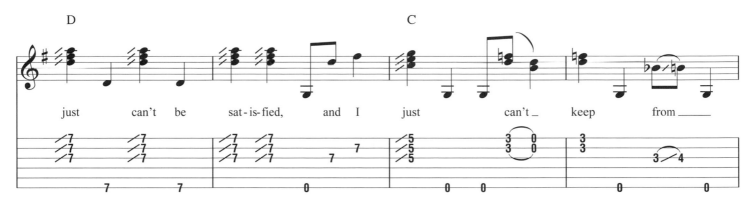

just can't be sat-is-fied, and I just can't keep from

cry - in'.   2. Well, ___ I ____
                     4. *See additional lyrics*

Verse

feel like snap-pin' pis - tol in your face.

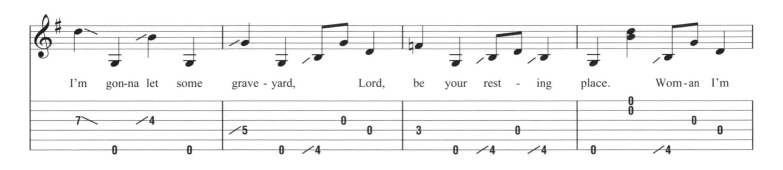

I'm gon-na let some grave - yard, Lord, be your rest - ing place. Wom-an I'm

trou - bled,   I   be   all   wor - ried   in   mind.

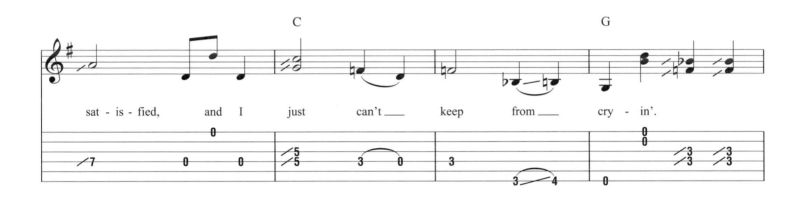

Well,   babe,   I   can   nev - er   be

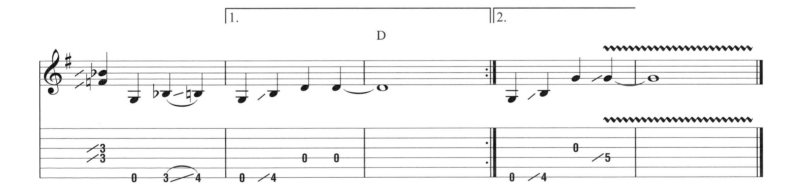

sat - is - fied,   and   I   just   can't ___   keep   from ___   cry - in'.

Additional Lyrics

3. Well, now all in my sleep, hear my doorbell ring,
   Looking for my baby, I couldn't see not a doggone thing.
   Woman, I was troubled, I was all worried in mind.
   Well, honey, I could never be satisfied,
   And I just couldn't keep from cryin'.

4. Well, I know my little old baby, she gonna jump and shout.
   That old train be late, man, Lord, and I come walking out.
   I be troubled, I be all worried in mind.
   Well, honey, ain't no way in the world could we be satisfied,
   And I just can't keep from crying.

Old Joe Clark

Tennessee Folksong

One of the most popular fiddle tunes, "Old Joe Clark" goes back as far as the 1800s, and the ninety or more verses indicate its possible origin as a children's song. There are many conflicting stories of a real Joe Clark: he was a civil war soldier from Kentucky, or a murderer from Virginia, or somebody else entirely. Bluegrassers rarely sing the verses; they play it as an instrumental in the key of A. (A typical verse: "I wouldn't marry an old schoolteacher, tell you the reason why: She'd blow her nose in old cornbread and call it pumpkin pie.")

G tuning:
(low to high) G-B-D-G-B-D

Key of A

I'm So Lonesome I Could Cry

Words and Music by Hank Williams

Hank Williams often called "I'm So Lonesome I Could Cry" his favorite record, and critics cite its lyrics to prove that country music can be beautiful poetry. Recorded in 1949, Williams wrote it as a poem for one of his "Luke the Drifter" recitations with musical background. Fortunately, he changed his mind, sang it to a beautiful melody, and made it one of country music's best-loved and most-recorded songs. It has been covered by such diverse artists as Al Green, Marty Robbins, Glen Campbell, Johnny Cash, the Cowboy Junkies, Leon Russell, B.J. Thomas, and Jerry Lee Lewis. The solo in this arrangement is similar to what was played on Williams' recording by the famous and influential steel player, Jerry Byrd.

C6 tuning:
(low to high) C-E-G-A-C-E

Key of E
Verse
Slow Waltz

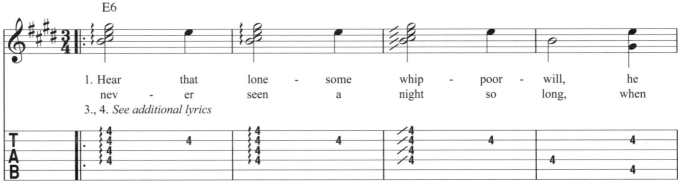

1. Hear that lone - some whip - poor - will, he
nev - er seen a night so long, when
3., 4. *See additional lyrics*

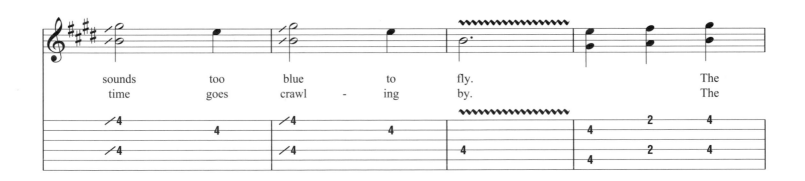

sounds too blue to fly. The
time goes crawl - ing by. The

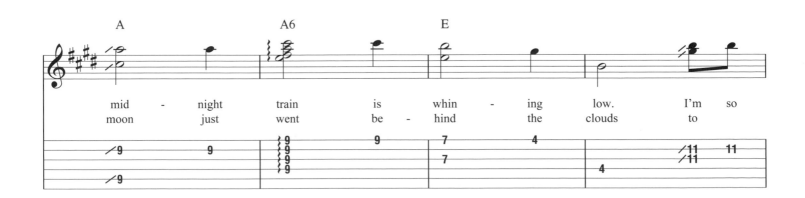

mid - night train is whin - ing low. I'm so
moon just went be - hind the clouds to

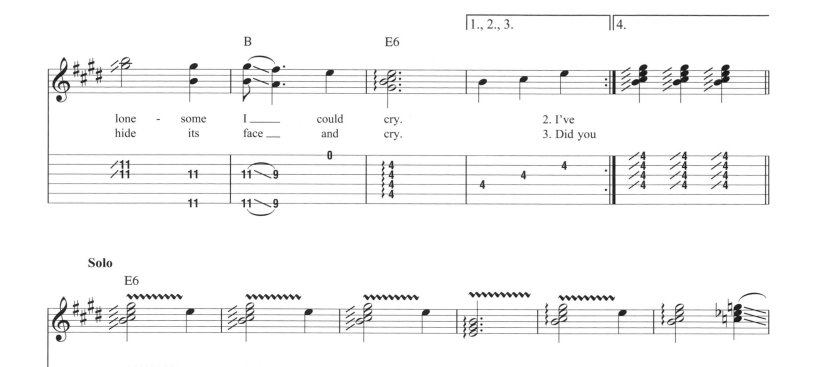

lone - some   I ___   could   cry.
hide   its   face ___   and   cry.
2. I've
3. Did you

Solo

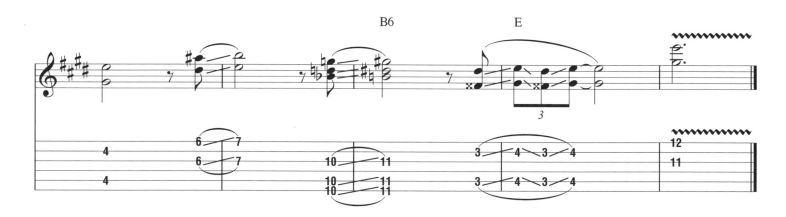

Additional Lyrics

3. Did you ever see a robin weep when leaves begin to die?
   Like me, he's lost the will to live. I'm so lonesome I could cry.

4. The silence of a falling star lights up a purple sky,
   And as I wonder where you are, I'm so lonesome I could cry.

I'm Thinking Tonight of My Blue Eyes

Words and Music by A.P. Carter

In 1929, when the Carter Family recorded "I'm Thinking Tonight of My Blue Eyes," they said it was a song they had heard all their lives. It had already been recorded by several other country artists (with different titles such as "Thrills I Can't Forget" from 1925) and would become one of the most popular melodies in country music. Learn to play it, and you're learning the solo to a list of popular country tunes that share almost the exact same melody, including "The Prisoner's Song," "The Great Speckled Bird," "The Wild Side of Life," and Kitty Wells' answer to the latter: "It Wasn't God Who Made Honky Tonk Angels."

The verse and chorus share the same melody and chords. In this arrangement, the chorus is played in a lower register than the verse.

C6 tuning:
(low to high) C-E-G-A-C-E

Key of F

Chorus

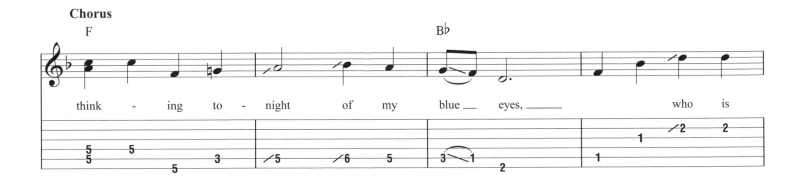

think - ing to - night of my blue eyes, who is

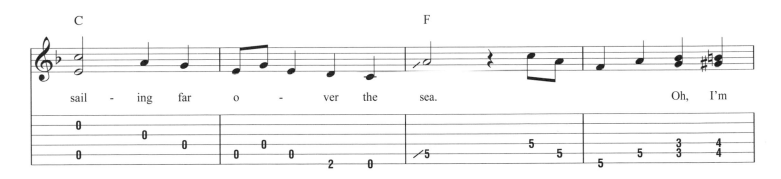

sail - ing far o - ver the sea. Oh, I'm

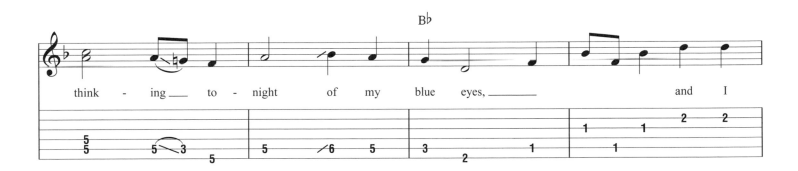

think - ing to - night of my blue eyes, and I

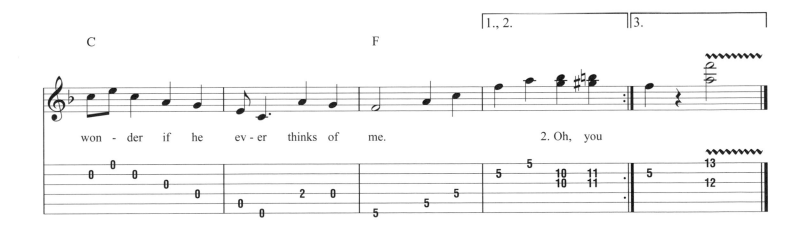

won - der if he ev - er thinks of me. 2. Oh, you

Additional Lyrics

2. Oh, you told me once, dear, that you loved me. You said that we never would part.
   But a link in the chain has been broken, leaves me with a sad and aching heart.

3. When the cold, cold grave shall enclose me, will you come, dear, and shed just one tear,
   And say to the strangers around you, "A poor heart you have broken lies here"?

Keep Your Lamp Trimmed and Burning

Words and Music by Blind Willie Johnson

Many blues singers of the late 1920s and early 1930s included traditional gospel songs in their repertoire (Mississippi Fred McDowell, Son House, Mississippi John Hurt). Then there were blues singers who almost exclusively performed gospel music (they should be called gospel singers!), like Reverend Gary Davis and Blind Willie Johnson. Johnson recorded "Keep Your Lamp Trimmed and Burning" in 1928, playing, as he always did, in open D tuning with a slide. Many passages in the Bible mention keeping a lamp trimmed, i.e., preparing the wick of an oil lamp, so as to be prepared for a "visitation."

This arrangement of the tune imitates Johnson's fingerpicking style, in which the thumb plays alternating D bass notes while the fingers pick the melody on the treble strings. Just as Muddy Waters did in "I Can't Be Satisfied," Johnson played the song's melody while singing it. The melody implies chord changes, but Johnson chose not to play them.

D tuning:
(low to high) D-A-D-F#-A-D

Key of D

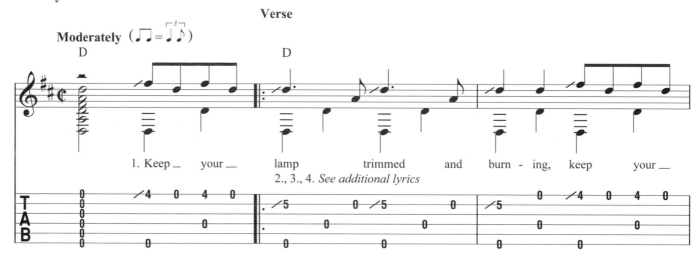

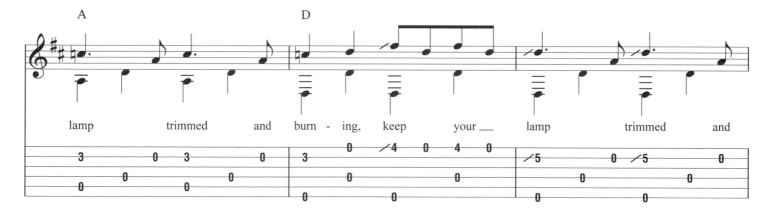

don't   get   wor - ried, _____ sis - ter don't   get

wor - ried, _____ sis - ter don't   get   wor - ried, _____ for the

work is _____ al - most _____ done.   2. Keep__ your __ done.

Additional Lyrics

2. Keep your lamp trimmed and burning, keep your lamp trimmed and burning,
   Keep your lamp trimmed and burning, oh, see what the Lord has done.
   Brother, don't get worried, brother, don't get worried,
   Brother, don't get worried, for the work is almost done.

3. Heaven journey's gone before, heaven journey's gone before,
   Heaven journey's gone before, oh, see what the Lord has done.
   Elder, don't get worried, elder, don't get worried,
   Elder, don't get worried, for the work is almost done.

4. Almost over, almost over,
   Almost over, see what the Lord has done.
   Brother, don't get worried, brother, don't get worried,
   Brother, don't get worried, for the work is almost done.

Little Red Rooster

Words and Music by Willie Dixon

The prolific bass player/songwriter Willie Dixon wrote this popular blues, and Howlin' Wolf recorded it in 1961, playing slide guitar while singing the tune. The Rolling Stones released their version as a single in 1964 and, despite the fact that it was a slow, straight blues (and not a pop offering), it reached #1 on the charts.

G tuning:
(low to high) G-B-D-G-B-D

Key of G
Intro
Moderately slow

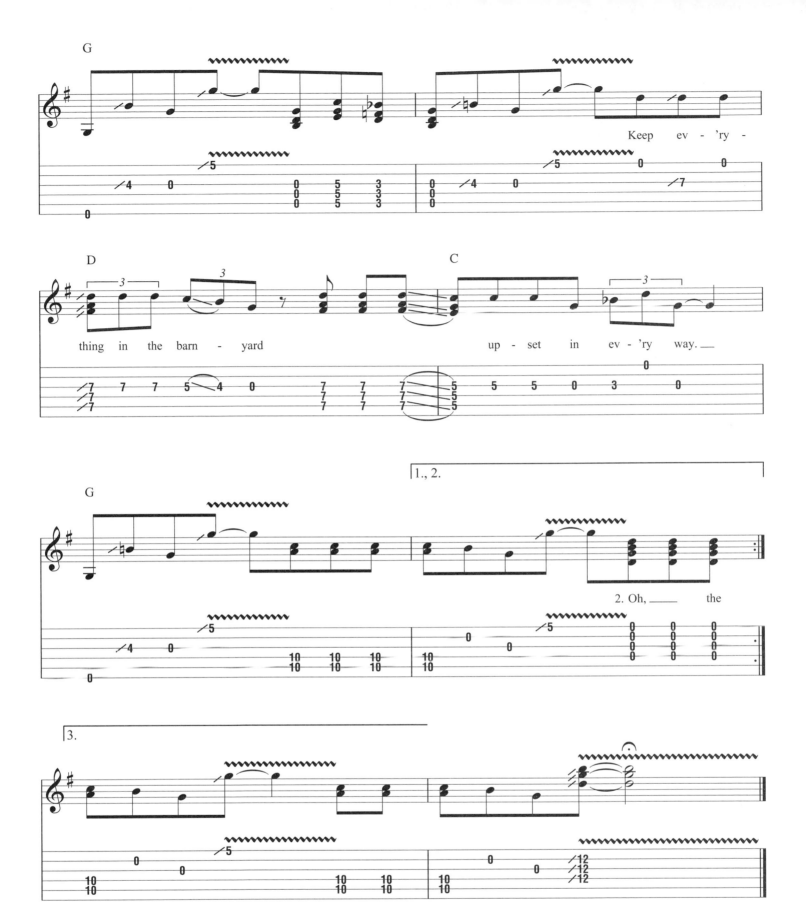

Additional Lyrics

2. Oh, the dogs begin to barkin', hounds begin to howl.
   Oh, the dogs begin to barkin', hounds begin to howl.
   Oh, watch out strange kin people, the little red rooster's on the prowl.

3. If you see my little red rooster, please drive him home.
   If you see my little red rooster, please drive him home.
   Ain't been no peace in the barnyard since the little red rooster been gone.

A Maiden's Prayer

Words and Music by Bob Wills

Bob Wills heard an old (1856) Polish piano exercise being played on a fiddle and recorded a western swing version of it in 1935. A few years later, he added lyrics. It has become a standard for fiddlers, and many country vocalists have recorded it as well.

C6 tuning:
(low to high) C-E-G-A-C-E

Key of A

Verse

Slow Country Shuffle

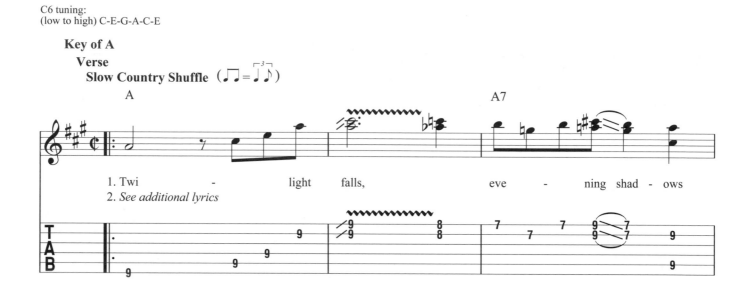

1. Twi - light falls, eve - ning shad - ows
2. *See additional lyrics*

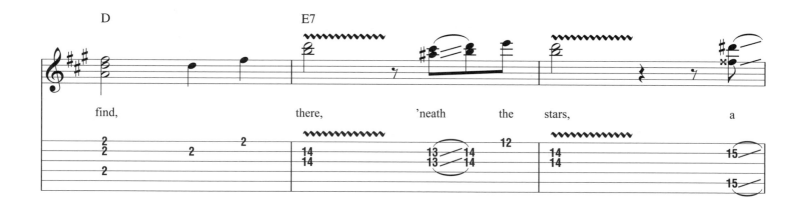

find, there, 'neath the stars, a

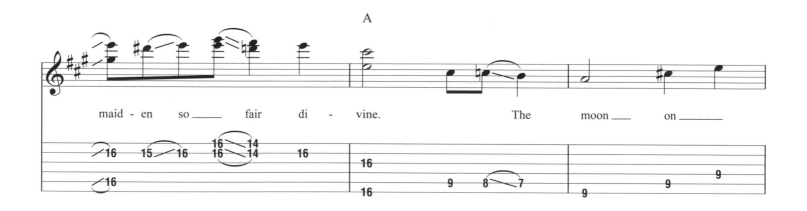

maid - en so ___ fair di - vine. The moon ___ on ___

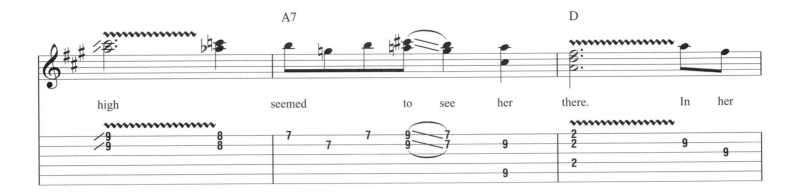

high   seemed   to   see   her   there.   In   her

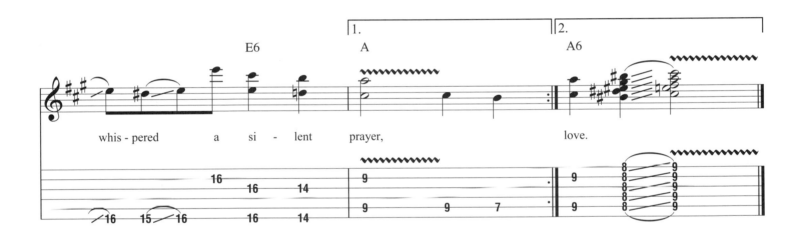

eyes ___ was a light, shin - ing ev - er so ___ bright, as she

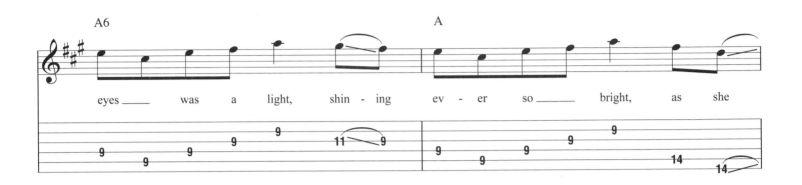

whis - pered   a   si - lent   prayer,   love.

Additional Lyrics

2. Ev'ry word revealed an empty, broken heart;
    Broken by fate that holds them so far apart.
    Lonely there she kneels, and tells the stars above,
    In her arms he belongs, then her pray'r is a song,
    Her unending song of love.

Mother's Children Have a Hard Time

Words and Music by Blind Willie Johnson

The above title is a misnomer: someone misunderstood Blind Willie Johnson singing "Motherless children have a hard time when mother is dead," and copyrighted the tune with an incorrect title. Since Johnson, Reverend Gary Davis, and the Carter Family recorded similar versions of the gospel tune in the late 1920s, its origin is uncertain. Johnson fingerpicked his guitar bottleneck style, tuned to open D, and implied but did not play the chord changes. His alternating-thumb/bass style and overall arrangement adapts well to Dobro.

D tuning:
(low to high) D-A-D-F♯-A-D

Additional Lyrics

2. Nobody on earth can take a mother's place when, when mother is dead, Lord.
   Nobody on earth take mother's place when mother's dead.
   Nobody on earth takes mother's place.
   When you were startin', paved the way.
   Nobody treats you like mother will when…

3. Your wife or husband may be good to you, when mother is dead, Lord.
   They'll be good to you, mother's dead.
   A wife or your husband may be good to you,
   But better than nothing they'll prove untrue.
   Nobody treats you like mother will when, when mother is dead, Lord.

4. Well, some people say that sister will do, when mother is dead.
   …That sister will do when mother's dead.
   Some people say that sister will do,
   But, as soon as she's married, she'll turn her back on you.
   Nobody treats you like mother will.

5. And father will do the best he can, when mother is dead, Lord.
   Well, the best he can when mother is dead.
   Father will do the best he can,
   So many things a father can't understand.
   Nobody treats you like mother will.

San Antonio Rose

from SAN ANTONIO ROSE

By Bob Wills

Bob Wills wrote his signature song, "San Antonio Rose," as an instrumental in 1938. Lyrics were added a few
years later and the title became "New San Antonio Rose." The bridge changes keys, going up a fifth (from A to E).

C6 tuning:
(low to high) C-E-G-A-C-E

Key of A

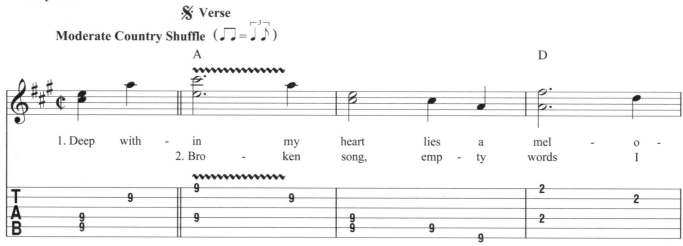

ry, be - neath the stars, all a - lone. ____
mo, and rose my rose of San An - tone. ____

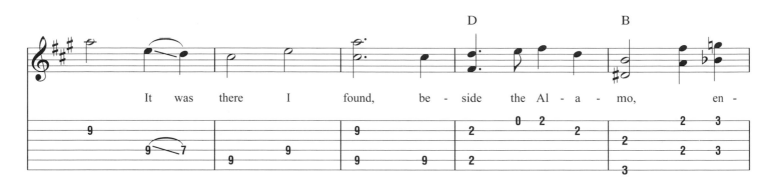

It was there I found, be - side the Al - a - mo, en -

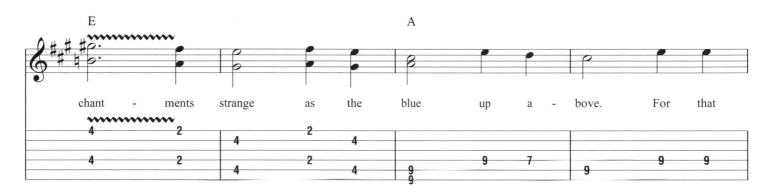

chant - ments strange as the blue up a - bove. For that

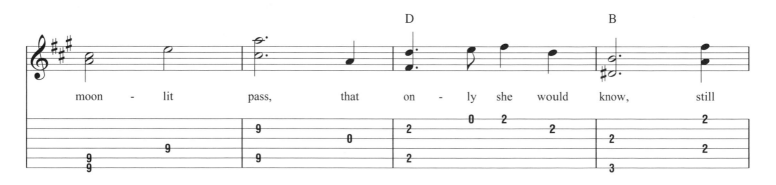

moon - lit pass, that on - ly she would know, still

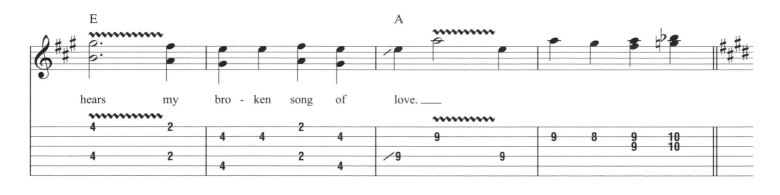

hears my bro - ken song of love. ____

Bridge

Moon in all your spen-dor, known on-ly to my heart,

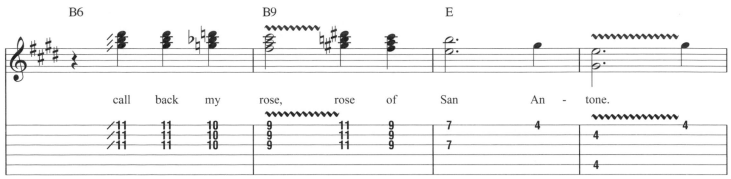

call back my rose, rose of San An-tone.

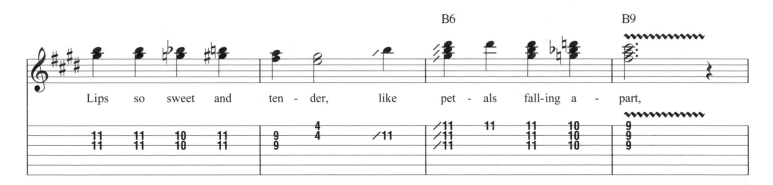

Lips so sweet and ten-der, like pet-als fall-ing a-part,

D.S. al Coda

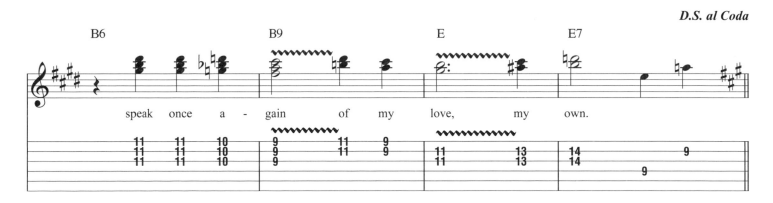

speak once a-gain of my love, my own.

Coda

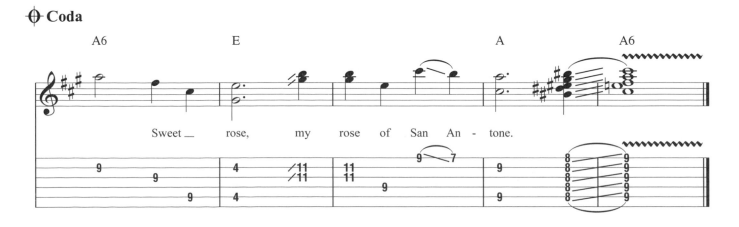

Sweet __ rose, my rose of San An-tone.

Panhandle Rag

Words and Music by Leon McAuliffe

On his western swing recordings, Bob Wills was often heard calling out "Take it away, Leon," to his steel guitarist, Leon McAuliffe. Leon helped popularize the steel guitar during his tenure with Wills, and he composed and recorded "Panhandle Rag" in 1949 when he was fronting his own band. Like his "Steel Guitar Rag," it has become an essential tune in the repertoire of steel guitar and Dobro players.

C6 tuning:
(low to high) C-E-G-A-C-E

Key of E

Pearly Shells
(Pupu 'O 'Ewa)

Words and Music by Webley Edwards and Leon Pober

The traditional Hawaiian song "Pearly Shells (Pupu 'O 'Ewa)" spoke of the discovery of pearl oysters at Pu'uloa, the Hawaiian name for (where else?) Pearl Harbor. Webley Edwards, a promoter of Hawaiian tourism and Hawaiian music, co-wrote English lyrics to the tune, creating what would become one of Don Ho's signature songs—and one of the most popular hapa-haole offerings. Like "Tiny Bubbles," it's a natural for audience participation, as each phrase is followed by a pause in which the audience can sing a repeated phrase: *Singer: "Pearly shells,"* Audience: *"Pearly shells."*

C6 tuning:
(low to high) C-E-G-A-C-E

Key of G

Bridge

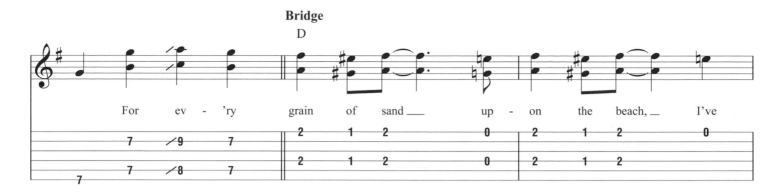

For ev - 'ry grain of sand ___ up - on the beach, ___ I've

got a kiss ___ for you, and I've got more left o - ver

D.S. al Coda

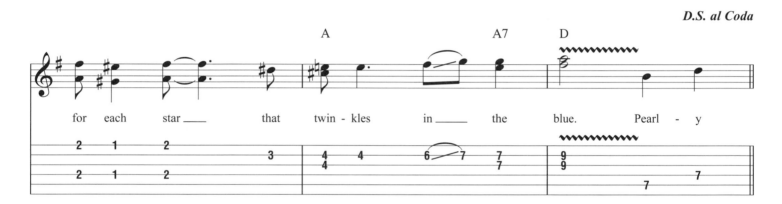

for each star ___ that twin - kles in ___ the blue. Pearl - y

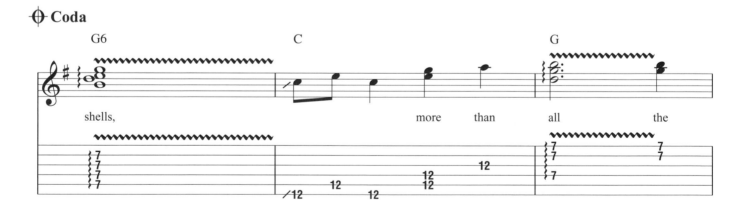

shells, more than all the

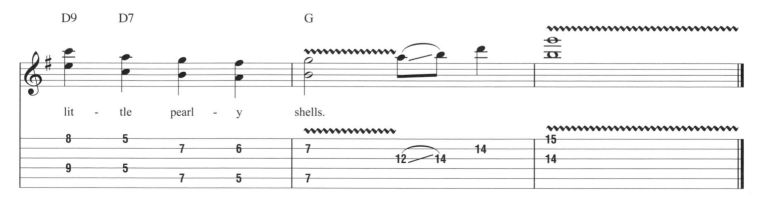

lit - tle pearl - y shells.

Pick Away

Words and Music by Gladys Flatt and Victor Jordan

Mike Auldridge was a founding member of one of the first "newgrass" groups, the Seldom Scene. The group broadened the repertoire of bluegrass in the 1970s, covered pop songs, and generally pushed the envelope beyond strictly traditional bluegrass. One of the most admired Dobro players of all time, Auldridge learned from Josh Graves (from whom he bought his first Dobro), and developed his own style, which influenced later pickers like Jerry Douglas. His instrumental, "Pick Away," has become a standard for Dobroists. Note the many three-finger, banjo-like rolls (they're really thumb and two fingers).

G tuning:
(low to high) G-B-D-G-B-D

Key of G

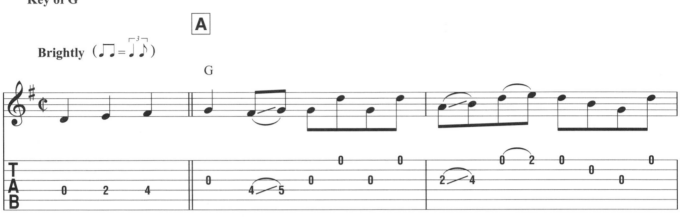

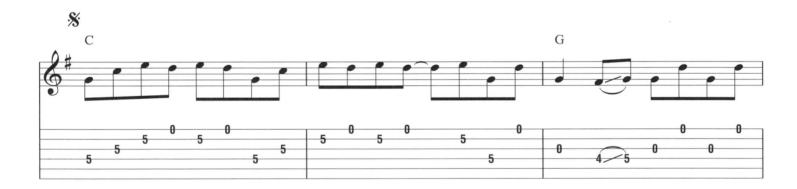

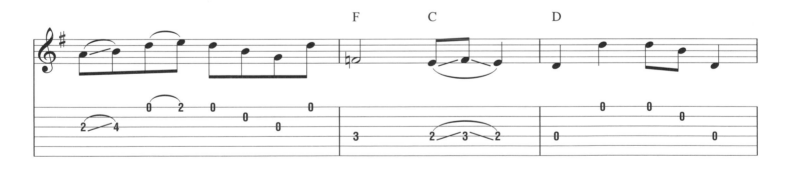

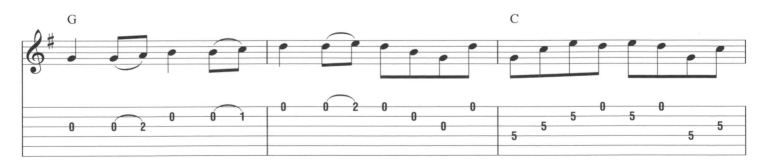

To Coda ⊕

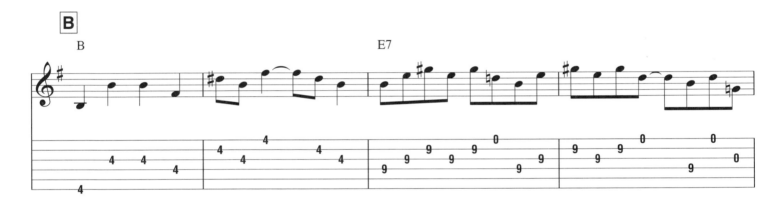

B

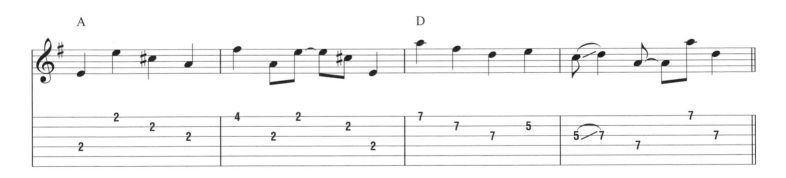

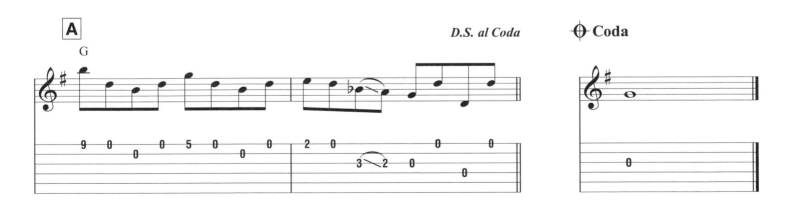

A

D.S. al Coda   ⊕ **Coda**

Roll in My Sweet Baby's Arms

Words and Music by Lester Flatt

Posey Rorer, Buster Carter, and Preston Young recorded a version of this old folk song in 1931.
Flatt and Scruggs' 1951 arrangement has been covered by countless bluegrass and country artists.

G tuning:
(low to high) G-B-D-G-B-D

Key of G
Verse
Bright Two-Beat

1. Ain't gon - na work on the rail - road, _____
2., 3., 4. *See additional lyrics*

ain't gon - na work on the farm, gon - na

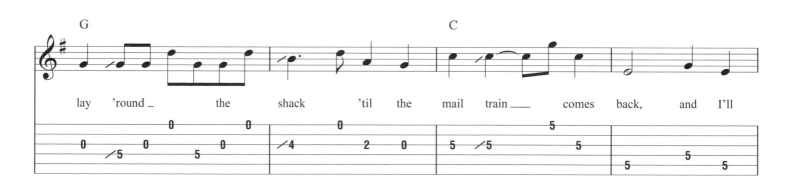

lay 'round _ the shack 'til the mail train ___ comes back, and I'll

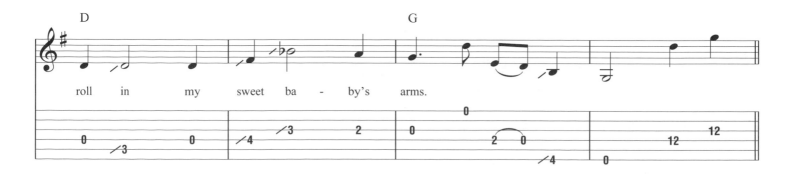

roll in my sweet ba - by's arms.

Chorus

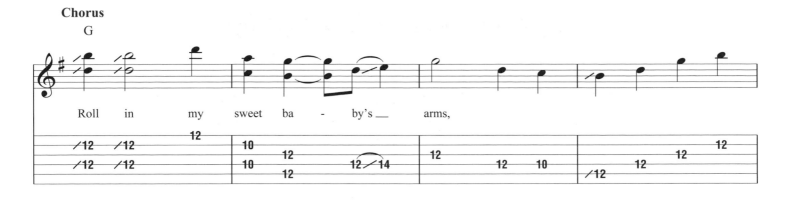

Roll in my sweet ba - by's __ arms,

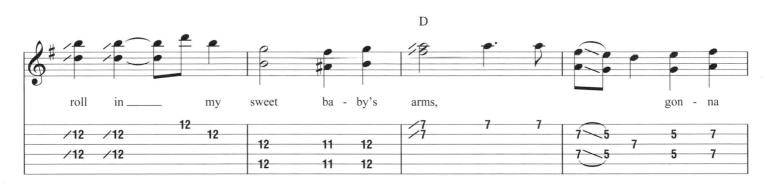

roll in __ my sweet ba - by's arms, gon - na

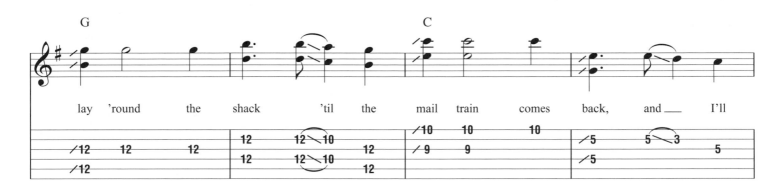

lay 'round the shack 'til the mail train comes back, and __ I'll

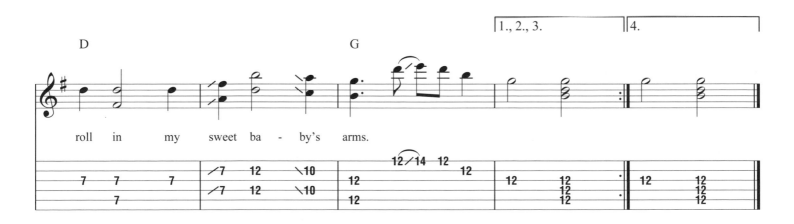

roll in my sweet ba - by's arms.

Additional Lyrics

2. Now, where was you last Friday night while I was lyin' in jail?
Walkin' the streets with another man, you wouldn't even go my bail.

3. I know your parents don't like me, they drove me away from your door.
If I had my life to live over again, I'd never go there anymore.

4. Mama's a beauty operator, sister can weave and can spin.
Dad's got an interest in the old cotton mill, just watch the money roll in.

Rollin' and Tumblin'

Words and Music by McKinley Morganfield

There are many recorded versions of this blues standard starting with Willie "Hambone" Newbern's 1929 "Roll and Tumble Blues" (he probably used a hambone for a slide); Robert Johnson's 1936 variation added a whole new set of lyrics (called "If I Had Possession Over Judgment Day"); and Muddy Waters recorded a 1950 rendering. There are notable rock versions by Eric Clapton (both electric with Cream and "unplugged"), Johnny Winter, Fleetwood Mac, and Bob Dylan to name just a few. Everyone puts their own spin on the tune, but most versions have the famous signature instrumental riff that repeats between vocal phrases and plays havoc with any attempt at a time signature: extra beats abound. Though usually played bottleneck guitar style, it adapts well to lap-style Dobro.

G tuning:
(low to high) G-B-D-G-B-D

Key of G

Verse

Bright Blues

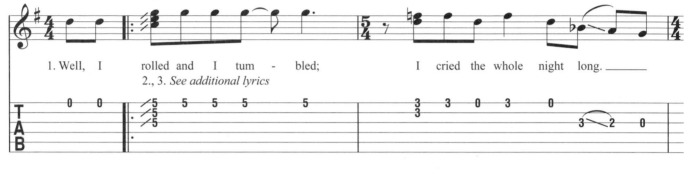

1. Well, I rolled and I tum-bled; I cried the whole night long.
2., 3. *See additional lyrics*

Well, I rolled and I tum-bled;

I cried the whole night long.

When I

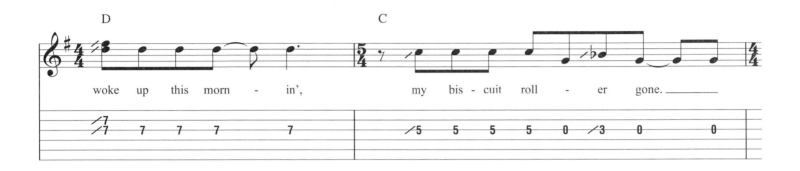

woke up this morn - in', my bis - cuit roll - er gone. _____

2. Well, I

Additional Lyrics

2. Well, I told my baby, before I left this town,
   Well, I told my baby, before I left this town,
   Well, don't you let nobody tear my barrelhouse down.

3. Well, if the river was whiskey, and I was a divin' duck,
   Well, if the river was whiskey, and I was a divin' duck,
   Well, I would dive to the bottom, never would come up.

Running on Faith

Words and Music by Jerry Lynn Williams

"Running on Faith" first appeared on Eric Clapton's critically acclaimed 1989 album, *Journeyman*. He reprised the song a few years later on the live, six-Grammy winning *Unplugged* album. He played slide guitar in open G tuning on both versions. On the *Unplugged* video, we see Clapton sliding on a Dobro, played upright rather than lap-style. The following arrangement mimics his playing.

G tuning:
(low to high) G-B-D-G-B-D

Key of G

Verse

Moderate Rock Ballad

1. Late - ly I've been run - ning on faith. ___
2. Late - ly I've been talk - ing in my sleep. ___
3. *See additional lyrics*

What else can a poor boy do? ___ But my
Can't im - agine what I'd have to say. ___ Ex - cept my

To Coda ⊕

world ___ will be right   when love comes ___ o - ver
world ___ will be right   when love comes ___ back your

1.

me.
way.

Salty Dog Blues

Words and Music by Wiley A. Morris and Zeke Morris

There are bluesy recordings of "Salty Dog Blues" from as early as the 1920s (Papa Charlie Jackson, Clara Smith, and others), but the 1945 Morris Brothers version was the model for Flatt and Scruggs' 1950 recording and their arrangement is covered by bluegrass bands. Earl Scruggs may have brought the tune to his band (Flatt and Scruggs and the Foggy Mountain Boys), as he played with the Morris Brothers prior to his stint with Bill Monroe and later collaboration with Lester Flatt.

G tuning:
(low to high) G-B-D-G-B-D

Key of G

Verse

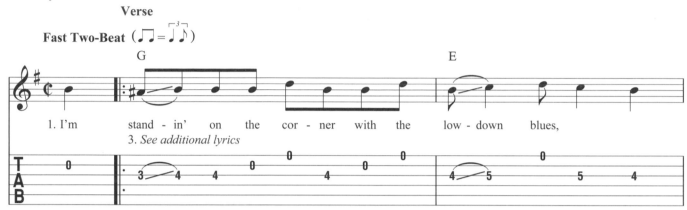

1. I'm standin' on the corner with the low-down blues,
3. *See additional lyrics*

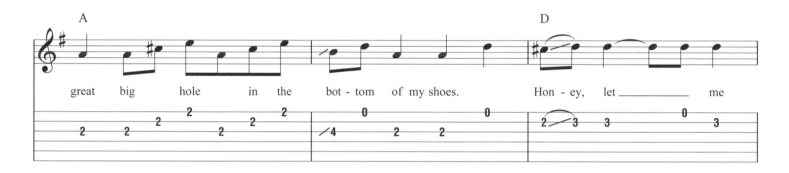

great big hole in the bottom of my shoes. Hon-ey, let _____ me

be your salt-y dog.

Chorus

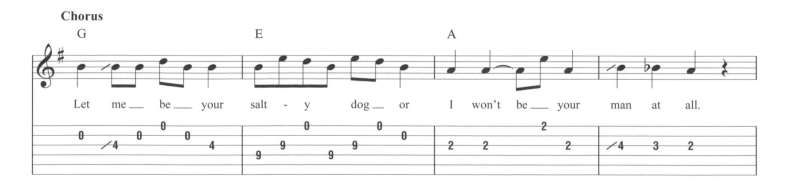

Let me __ be __ your salt-y dog __ or I won't be __ your man at all.

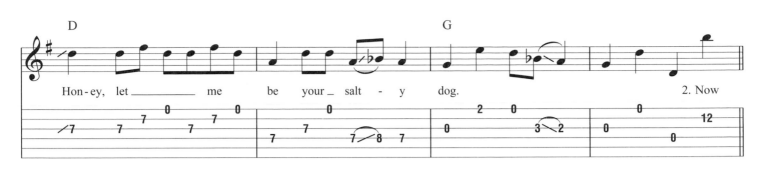

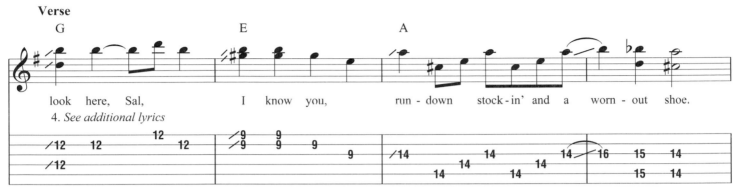

Verse

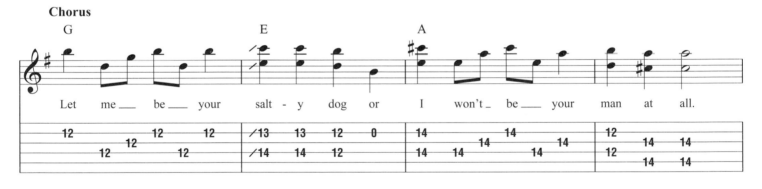

Chorus

Additional Lyrics

3. I was down in the wildwood settin' on a log,
   Finger on the trigger and an eye on the hog.
   Honey, let me be your salty dog.

4. I pulled the trigger and the gun said, "Go,"
   Shot fell over in Mexico.
   Honey, let me be your salty dog.

Sleepwalk
(Instrumental Version)

By Santo Farina, John Farina and Ann Farina

Brooklyn's Farina Brothers, Santo and Johnny, co-wrote this sleepy tune with their sister Ann. It went to #1 in 1959, when rock instrumentals were in vogue. The opening bars sound very much like Sigmund Romberg's "Softly, as in a Morning Sunrise." Santo played his solo on an eight-stringed lap steel in a C#m7 tuning. This arrangement is in standard C6 and closely resembles his playing. To play the artificial harmonics (indicated as "A.H.") in the tune's Intro and final bars, touch the strings with the palm of your picking hand, twelve frets above the fretted string. Since the bar is "fretting" the first string at the 3rd fret, touch the first string at the 15th fret with your palm . . . tricky, but effective once you master it.

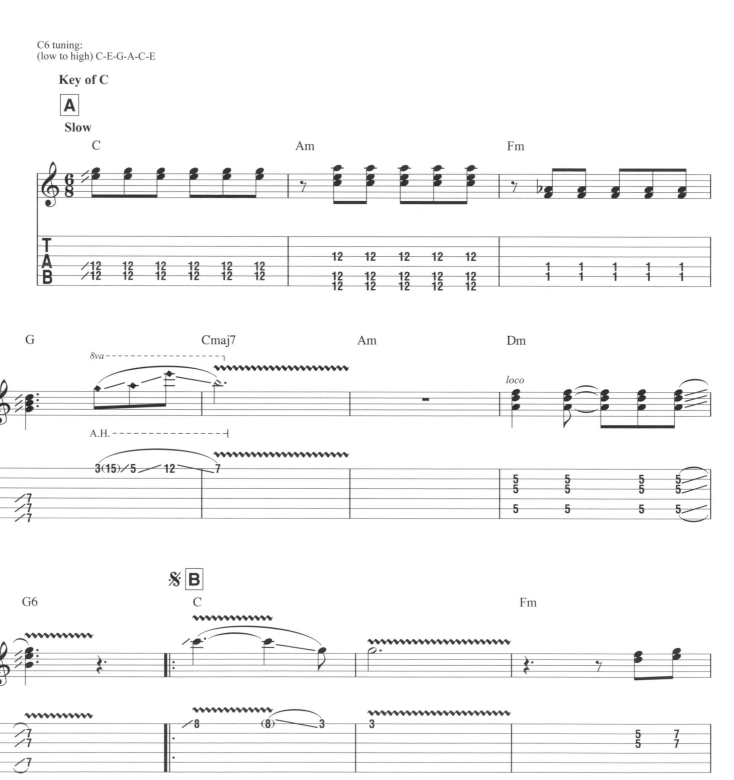

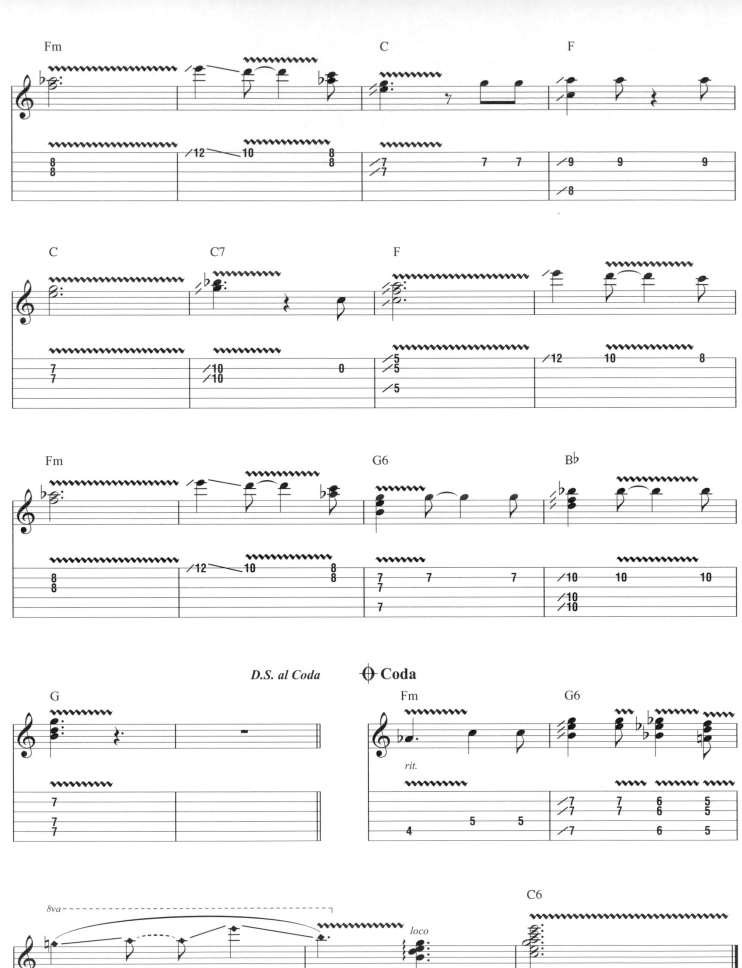

D.S. al Coda   ⊕ **Coda**

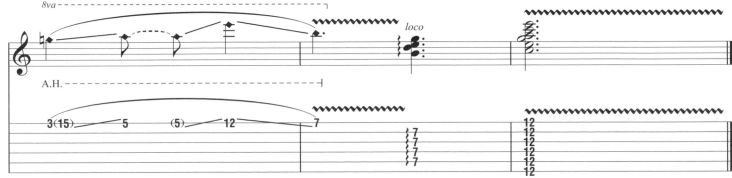

Smoke on the Water

Words and Music by Ritchie Blackmore, Ian Gillan, Roger Glover, Jon Lord and Ian Paice

Deep Purple's 1972 hit features one of the most iconic rock riffs of all time. However, most people play it incorrectly, according to lead guitarist Ritchie Blackmore who created it. (It's supposed to be played on a pair of strings in fourths, not fifths.) The song chronicles an actual event: a fire that broke out during a Mothers of Invention concert in Switzerland at a casino in which Deep Purple was scheduled to record the next day. They watched the fire from their hotel windows. "Funky Claude" was Claude Nobs, director of the Montreaux Jazz Festival who helped audience members evacuate the burning building.

G tuning:
(low to high) G-B-D-G-B-D

Key of G

Intro

Moderate Rock

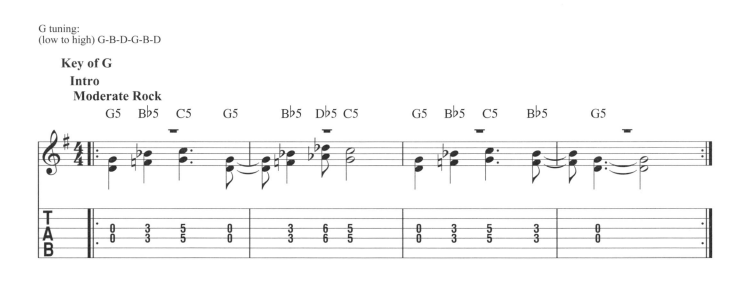

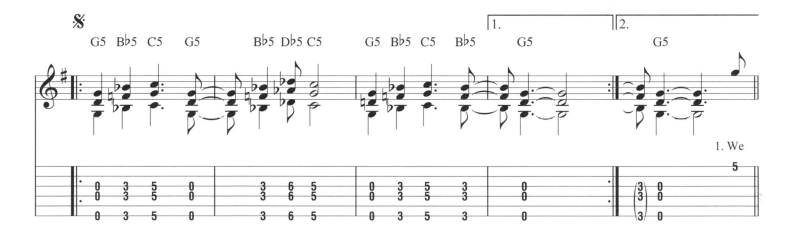

Verse

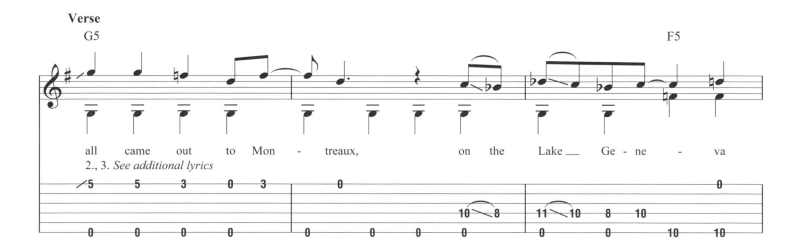

all came out to Mon - treaux, on the Lake ___ Ge - ne - va

2., 3. See additional lyrics

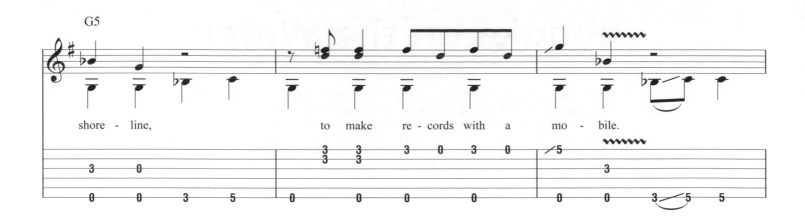

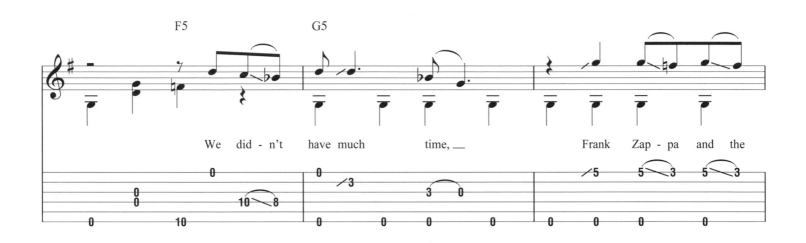

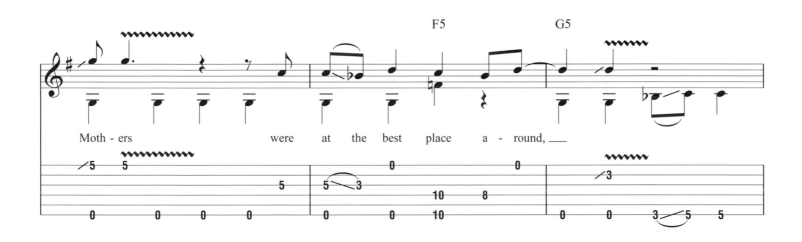

Additional Lyrics

2. They burned down the gambling house, it died with an awful sound.
   Funky Claude was running in and out, pulling kids out the ground.
   When it all was over, we had to find another place.
   But Swiss time was running out, it seemed that we would lose the race.

3. We ended up at the Grand Hotel, it was empty, cold, and bare.
   But with the Rolling truck Stones thing just outside, making our music there.
   With a few red lights and a few old beds, we made a place to sweat.
   No matter what we get out of this, I know, I know we'll never forget.

Statesboro Blues

Words and Music by Willie McTell

Statesboro is near Macon, Georgia, and the excellent Georgia-born bluesman, Blind Willie McTell, recorded his "Statesboro Blues" in 1928. His fingerpicking performance of the song, played on a twelve-string guitar (probably in open D tuning) is one of the most brilliant recordings of the era. About fifty years later, Taj Mahal recorded a popular cover of the tune, and The Allman Brothers' live 1971 *At Fillmore East* recording included yet another hit version. McTell was immortalized in Bob Dylan's song, "Blind Willie McTell."

This arrangement features an alternating thumb/bass, similar to McTell's picking style. If you're not adept at this type of fingerpicking, it's helpful to learn the melody notes (stems up) first, ignoring the stems-down thumb notes. When you're familiar with the melody, add the thumb/bass . . . slowly but surely. This method applies to the Blind Willie Johnson tunes in this collection as well.

D tuning:
(low to high) D-A-D-F♯-A-D

Verse

Additional Lyrics

2. Mama died and left me reckless, my daddy died and left me wild, wild, wild.
Mother died and left me reckless, daddy died and left me wild, wild, wild.
No, I'm not good lookin' but I'm some sweet woman's angel child.

3. She's a mighty mean woman, do me this-a-way.
She's a mighty mean woman, do me this-a-way.
When I leave this town, pretty mama, going away to stay.

4. Once loved a woman, better than even I'd ever seen.
I once loved a woman, better than even I'd ever seen.
Treated me like I'm a king and she was a doggone queen.

6. Big Eighty left Savannah, Lord, and did not stop.
You ought to saw that colored fireman when he got that boiler hot.
You can reach over in the corner mama and hand me my travelin' shoes.
You know by that, I've got them Statesboro blues.

Steel Guitar Rag

Words by Merle Travis and Cliff Stone
Music by Leon McAuliffe

Leon McAuliffe was perhaps the first well-known steel guitarist, due to his excellent playing with Bob Wills
and His Texas Playboys. And McAuliffe's "Steel Guitar Rag" was the instrumental that made the steel famous—
even if it was mostly derived from Sylvester Weaver's 1927 bottleneck guitar instrumental, "Guitar Rag." (Okay,
Leon's third section of the three-part tune is significantly different from Sylvester's.)

D tuning:
(low to high) D-A-D-F#-A-D

Key of D

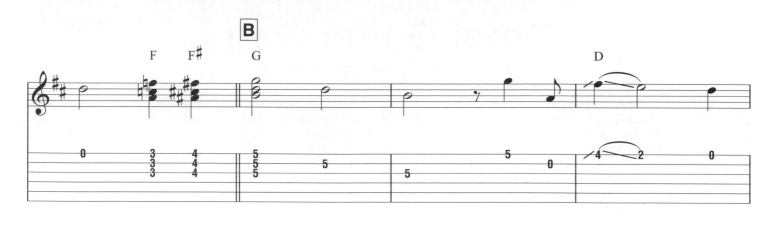

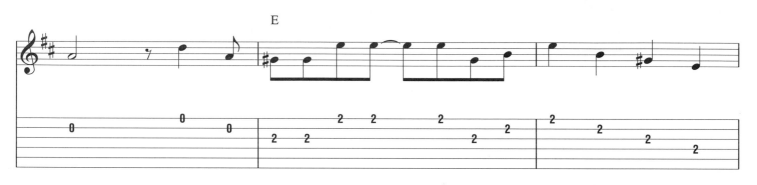

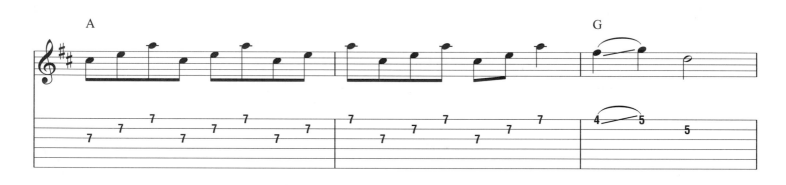

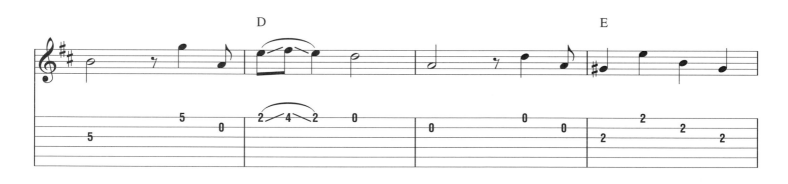

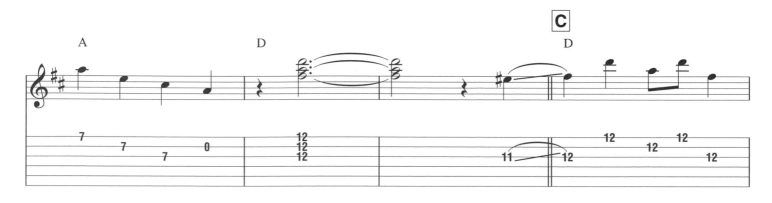

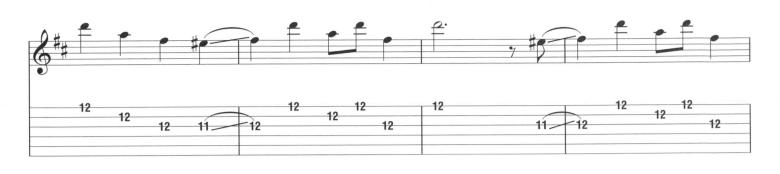

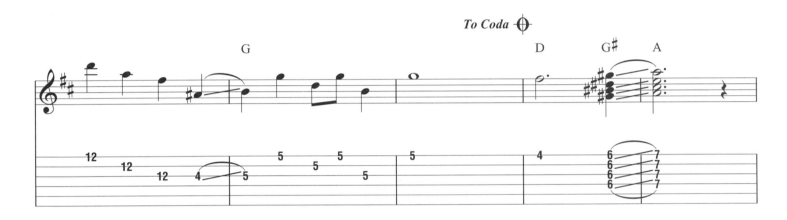

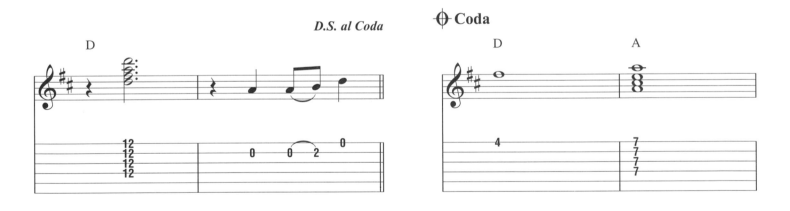

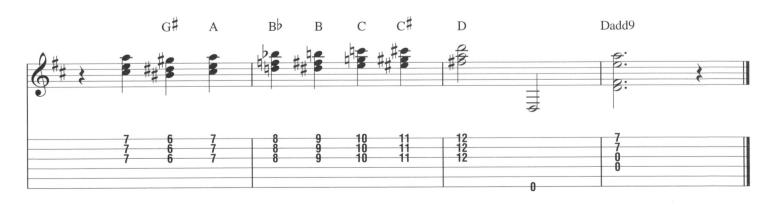

Sweet Leilani

Words and Music by Harry Owens

The Hawaiian name "Leilani" means "heavenly garland of flowers." The song was a big hit in 1937 when Bing Crosby sang it in the film, *Waikiki Wedding*, and it has become a standard in the pop Hawaiian repertoire, recorded by dozens of vocalists.

C6 tuning:
(low to high) C-E-G-A-C-E

Key of F

Verse

Slow

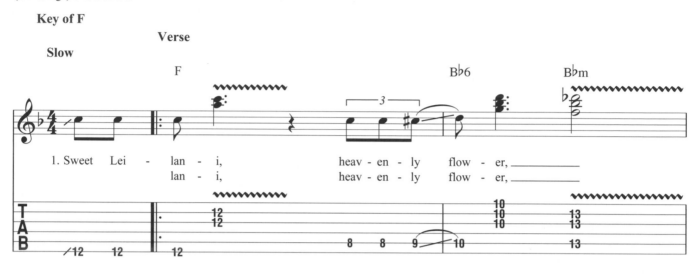

1. Sweet Lei - lan - i, heav - en - ly flow - er, ___
   lan - i, heav - en - ly flow - er, ___

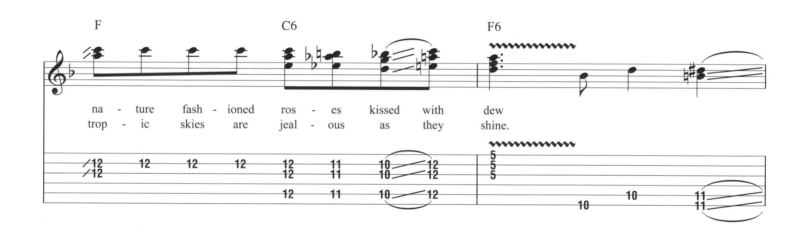

na - ture fash - ioned ros - es kissed with dew
trop - ic skies are jeal - ous as they shine.

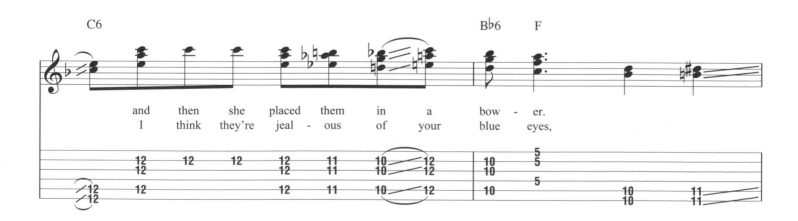

and then she placed them in a bow - er.
I think they're jeal - ous of your blue eyes,

Teach Your Children

Words and Music by Graham Nash

From the 1970 Crosby, Stills, Nash & Young album, *Déjà Vu*, this very popular tune featured Jerry Garcia on pedal steel.

Chorus

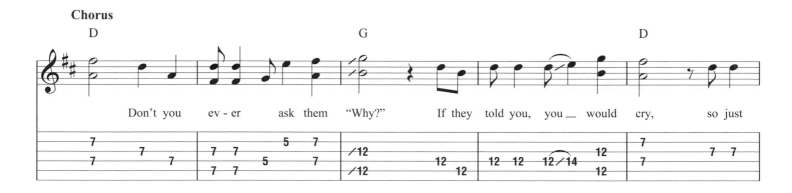

Don't you ev-er ask them "Why?" If they told you, you __ would cry, so just

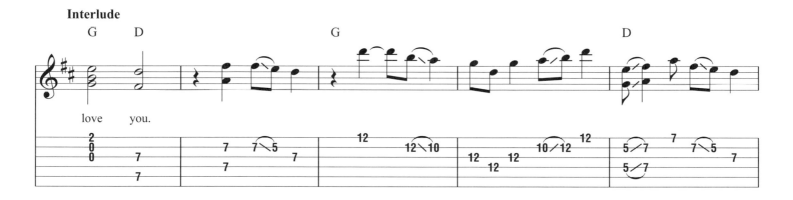

look at them _ and sigh, _____ and know they

Interlude

love you.

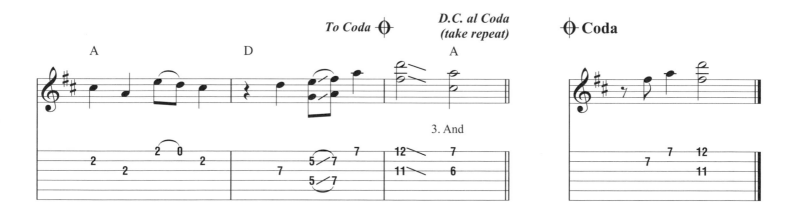

3. And

Additional Lyrics

3. And you of tender years, can't know the fears that your elders grew by.
   And so, please help them with your youth. They seek the truth before they can die.

4. Teach your parents well. Their children's hell will slowly go by.
   And feed them on your dreams. The one they pick's the one you'll know by.

Tiny Bubbles

Words and Music by Leon Pober

Audiences love Don Ho's signature song, "Tiny Bubbles," because it's phrased so that they can repeat every line: *Singer: "Tiny bubbles," Audience: "Tiny bubbles,"* etc. It charted in 1967 and has become one of the most popular hapa-haole songs.

G tuning:
(low to high) G-B-D-G-B-D

Key of G

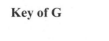

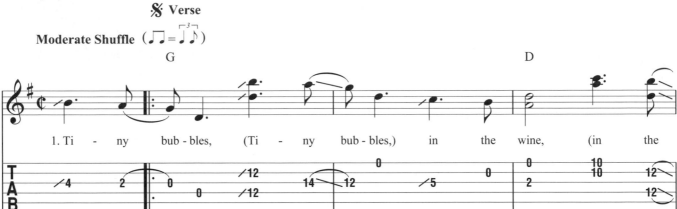

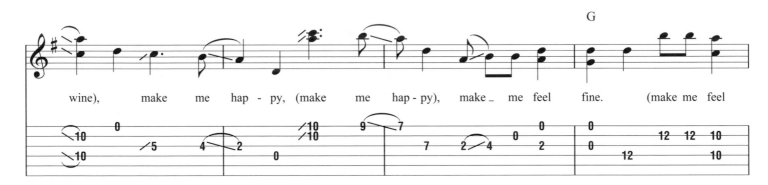

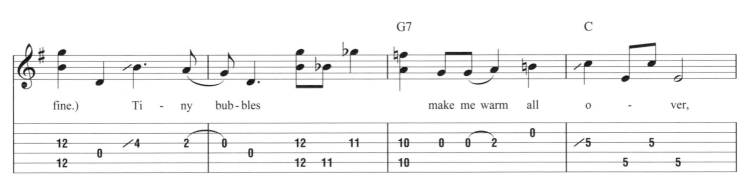

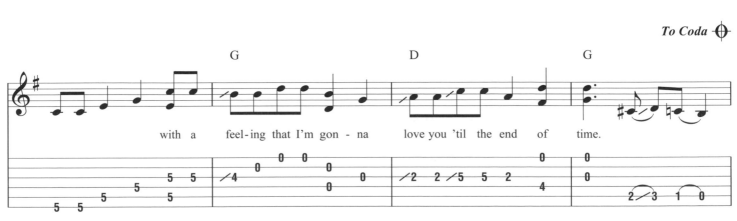

Traveling Riverside Blues

Words and Music by Robert Johnson

Recorded by Delta bluesman Robert Johnson in 1937 at his last session, this twelve-bar blues was given a creative treatment by Led Zeppelin. Their version of the tune quoted lyrics from several of Johnson's other songs. Johnson played the tune with a slide, in open G tuning, and capoed or tuned up three frets to an open B♭. He added extra bars and extra beats at will, though this arrangement adheres to the twelve-bar form. The towns mentioned in the song all lie along the Mississippi River; Friars Point is a small Mississippi town from which, in the 1930s, you could catch a ferry to cross the river to Helena, Arkansas—where liquor was legal!

G tuning:
(low to high) G-B-D-G-B-D

Key of G

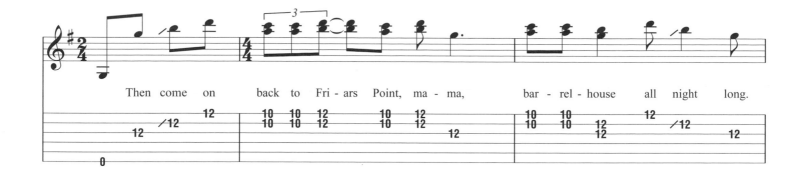

Then come on back to Fri - ars Point, ma - ma, bar - rel - house all night long.

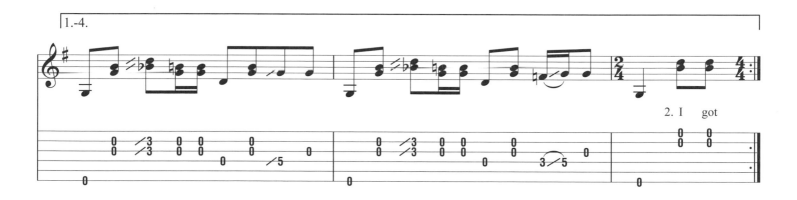

2. I got

Additional Lyrics

2. I got womens in Vicksburg, clean on into Tennessee.
   I got womens in Vicksburg, clean on into Tennessee.
   But my Friars Point rider, now, hops all over me.

3. I ain't gonna state no color, but her front teeth is crowned with gold.
   I ain't gonna state no color, but her front teeth is crowned with gold.
   She got a mortgage on my body, Lord, a lien on my soul.

4. Well, I'm going to Rosedale, gonna take my rider by my side.
   Well, I'm going to Rosedale, gonna take my rider by my side.
   We can still barrelhouse, baby, 'cause it's on the riverside.

5. You can squeeze my lemon 'til the juice run down my leg.
   You can squeeze my lemon 'til the juice run down my leg.
   But I'm going back to Friars Point, if I be rocking to my end.

Tumbling Tumbleweeds

Words and Music by Bob Nolan

Though many people know "Tumbling Tumbleweeds" because it begins and ends the movie *The Big Lebowski*, it was made famous in the early 1930s by the singing cowboy group, The Sons of the Pioneers. It became their theme song and one of the most famous cowboy songs, but it has been recorded by jazz artists like Harry James and Grant Green; pop stars like Frankie Laine, Bing Crosby, and The Supremes; actor Clint Eastwood; and punk rockers The Meat Puppets… among many others.

G tuning:
(low to high) G-B-D-G-B-D

Key of D

Intro

Moderately Slow Country Shuffle

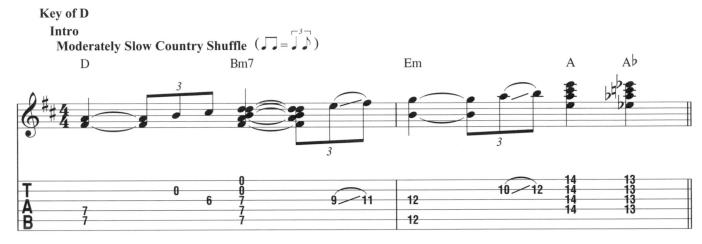

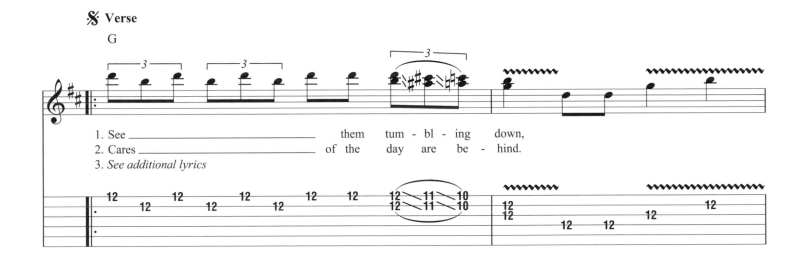

1. See _____ them tum - bl - ing down,
2. Cares _____ of the day are be - hind.
3. *See additional lyrics*

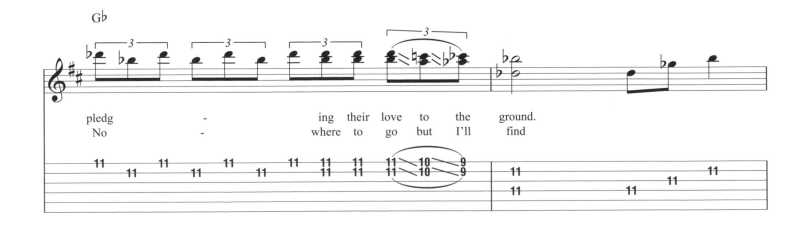

pledg - ing their love to the ground.
No - where to go but I'll find

Additional Lyrics

3. I'll keep rolling along, deep in my heart is a song.
   Here on the range I belong, drifting along with the tumbling tumbleweeds.

Wabash Cannonball

Words and Music by A.P. Carter

No one seems to know who Daddy Cleaton was (or Daddy Claxton, as he is called in most versions of the song) and many say the Wabash Cannonball was a mythical train. But the lyrics and tune come from a late 1800s song called "The Great Rock Island Route" about an actual train route that stretched across many states. In 1929, the Carter Family recorded a version of the song that had been rewritten as "The Wabash Cannonball" in 1904. Opry star Roy Acuff recorded the Carter Family version in 1936, with Pete Kirby (Bashful Brother Oswald) playing a famous Dobro solo, and it became Acuff's signature song. The words vary from one performer to another, but the lyrics here belong to the Carter Family.

This arrangement shows how to play the melody two ways: in first position, and up the neck. The higher register version includes no open strings, so it can be moved up or down the neck to play it in different keys.

G tuning:
(low to high) G-B-D-G-B-D

Key of G

Verse

Bright Two-Beat

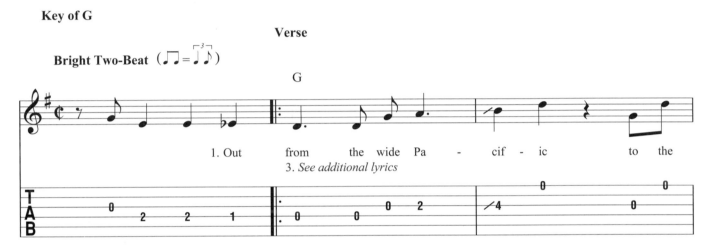

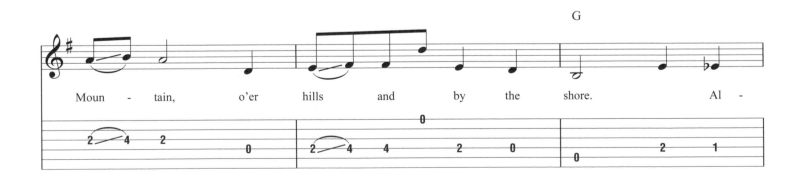

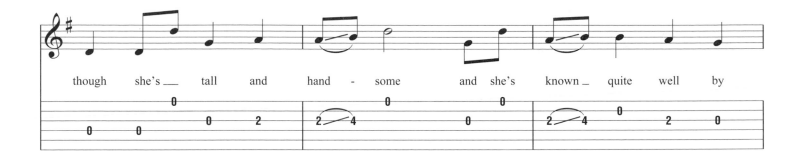

though she's ___ tall and hand - some and she's known ___ quite well by

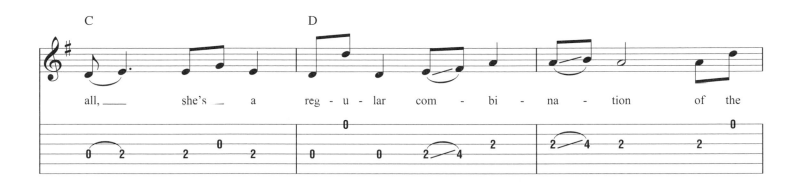

C   D

all, ___ she's ___ a reg - u - lar com - bi - na - tion of the

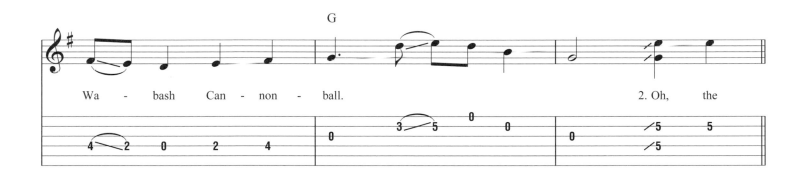

G

Wa - bash Can - non - ball.   2. Oh, the

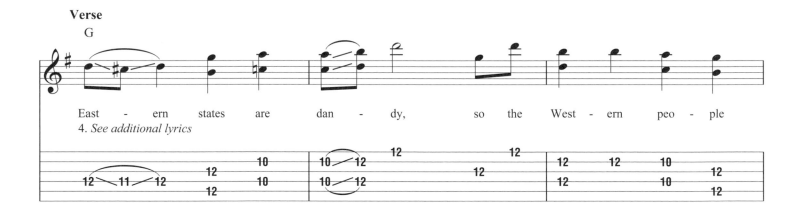

Verse

G

East - ern states are dan - dy, so the West - ern peo - ple

4. *See additional lyrics*

C   D

say, ___ Chi - ca - go, Rock Is - land, Saint

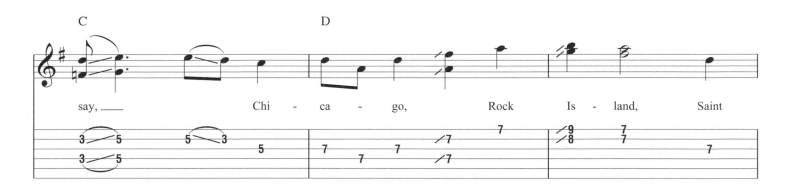

Lou - is   by   the   way. ___   To   the   lakes   of   Min - ne -

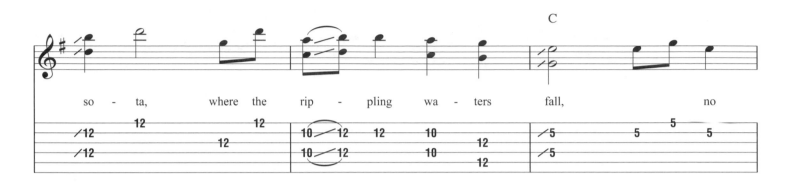

so - ta,   where   the   rip - pling   wa - ters   fall,   no

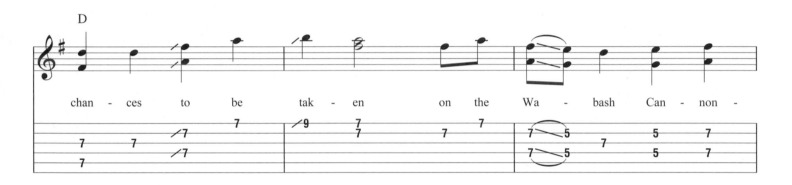

chan - ces   to   be   tak - en   on   the   Wa - bash   Can - non -

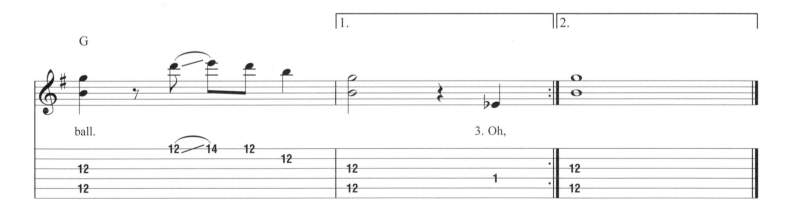

ball.   3. Oh,

Additional Lyrics

3. Oh, listen to the jingle, the rumble and the roar
   As she glides along the woodland, o'er hills and by the shore.
   She climbs the Flow'ry Mountain, hear the merry hobo squall,
   She glides along the woodland, the Wabash Cannonball.

4. Oh, here's old Daddy Cleaton, let his name forever be,
   And long be remembered in the courts of Tennessee.
   For he is a good ol' rounder 'til the curtain around him fall,
   He'll be carried back to victory on the Wabash Cannonball.

Wild Horses

Words and Music by Mick Jagger and Keith Richards

From the 1971 Rolling Stones album, *Sticky Fingers*, this is one of the Stones' most popular and prettiest ballads.

G tuning:
(low to high) G-B-D-G-B-D

Key of G
Verse
Slow Rock Ballad

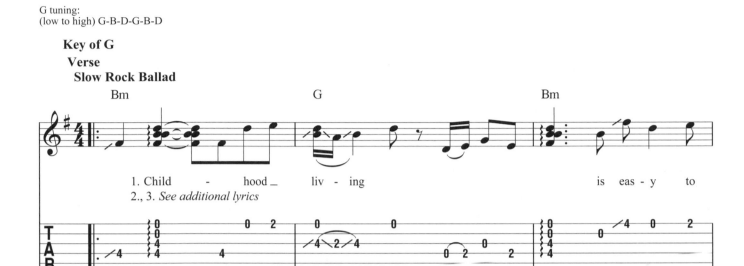

1. Child - hood __ liv - ing is eas - y to
2., 3. *See additional lyrics*

do. The things you __ want - ed,

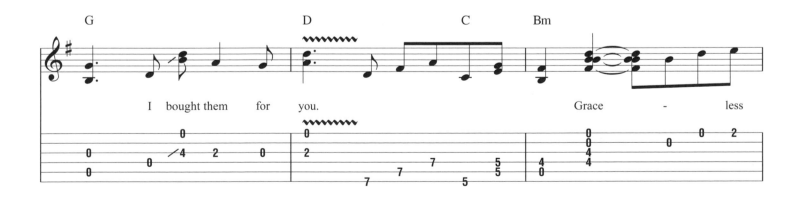

I bought them for you. Grace - less

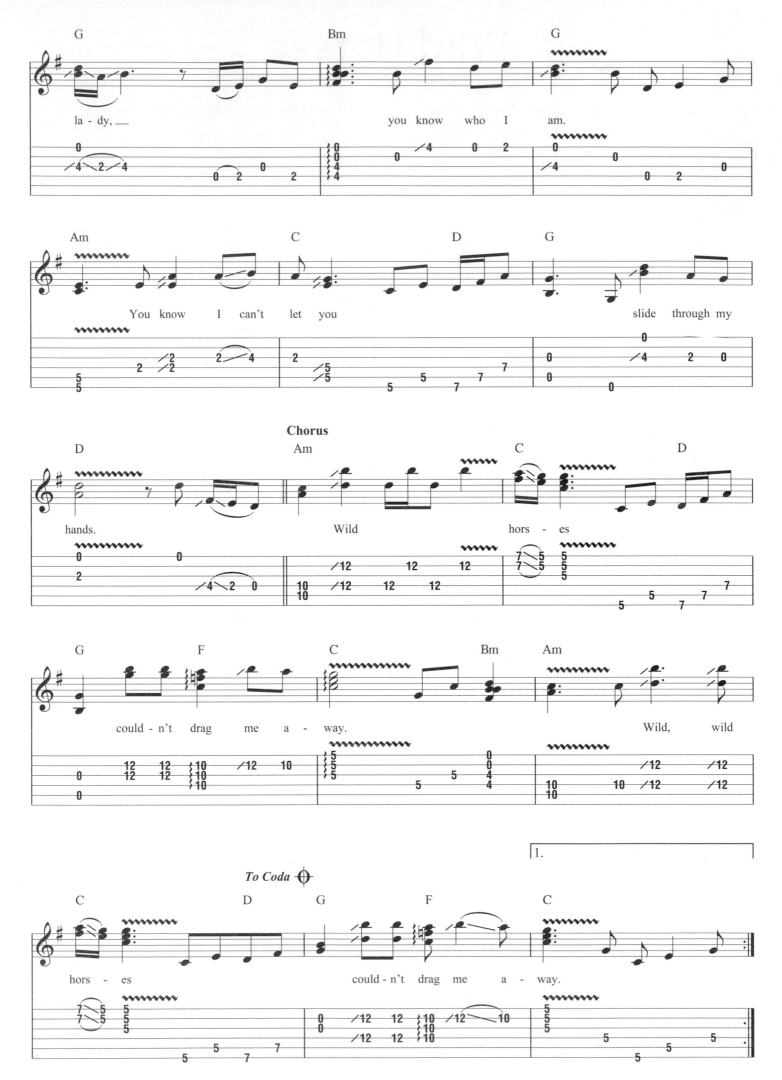

2.

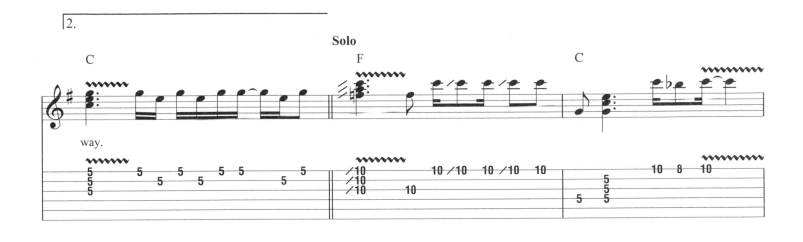

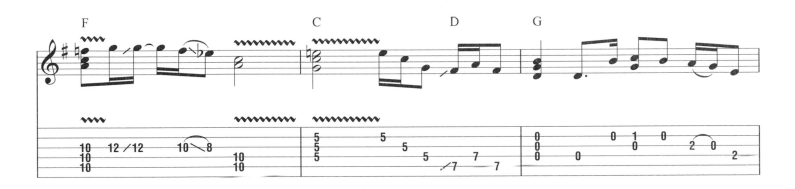

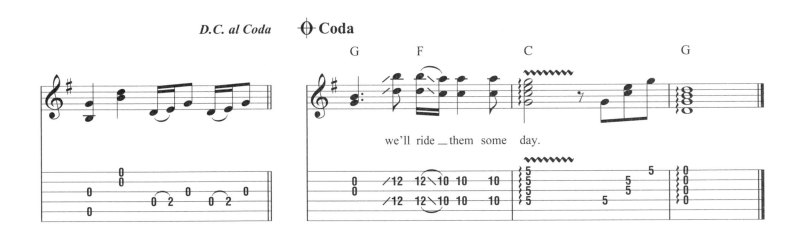

Additional Lyrics

2. I watched you suffer a dull aching pain. Now you've decided to show me the same.
   No sweeping exit or offstage lines could make me feel bitter or treat you unkind.

3. I know I've dreamed you a sin and a lie. I have my freedom, but I don't have much time.
   Faith has been broken, tears must be cried. Let's do some living after we die.

Wagon Wheel

Words and Music by Bob Dylan and Ketch Secor

Bob Dylan wrote the chorus ("Rock me mama…") for the 1973 film *Pat Garrett and Billy the Kid*, and twenty-five years later, Ketch Secor wrote the verses. In 2004, the song became a huge hit for Secor's group, Old Crow Medicine Show, and in 2013 it was a #1 hit for Darius Rucker. The song has become a campfire classic and a "Free Bird-level" request of bands all over the world. In this arrangement, the solo is played an octave higher than the verse and chorus.

G tuning:
(low to high) G-B-D-G-B-D

Key of A

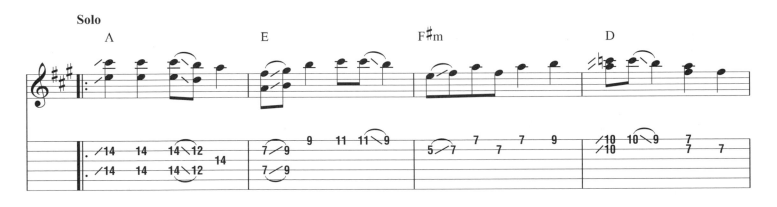

Additional Lyrics

3. Runnin' from the cold up in New England,
   I was born to be a fiddler in an old-time string band.
   My baby plays the guitar, I pick a banjo now.

4. Oh, the North country winters keep a-getting me now.
   Lost my money playin' poker so I had to up and leave,
   But I ain't a-turnin' back to livin' that old life no more.

5. Walkin' to the south out of Roanoke,
   I caught a trucker out of Philly, had a nice long toke.
   But he's a-headed west from the Cumberland Gap to Johnson City, Tennessee.

6. And I gotta get a move on before the sun.
   I hear my baby callin' my name and I know that she's the only one,
   And if I die in Raleigh at least I will die free.

Wayfaring Stranger

Southern American Folk Hymn

This gospel favorite goes back to the early 1800s, possibly earlier. It was sung at Appalachian revival services and spread west with the pioneers. Later, folksinger Burl Ives popularized it in the 1940s, followed by Joan Baez in the '60s, Emmylou Harris in the '80s, and Johnny Cash in 2000…and more recently, Ed Sheeran's cover has been widely viewed on YouTube. Bill Monroe recorded and performed many versions of it from the 1950s until his last years. In this arrangement, the C6 tuning makes it possible to play three-note minor chords.

C6 tuning:
(low to high) C-E-G-A-C-E

Key of Dm

Verse

Slow Shuffle

Chorus

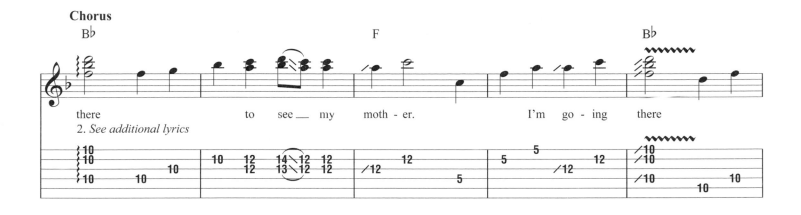

there to see __ my moth - er. I'm go - ing there

2. See additional lyrics

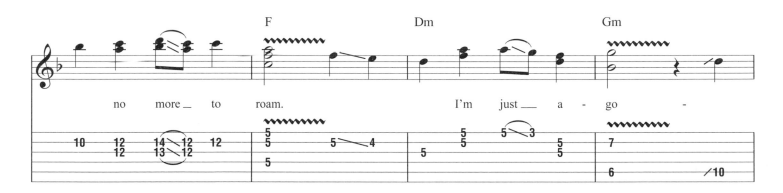

no more __ to roam. I'm just __ a go -

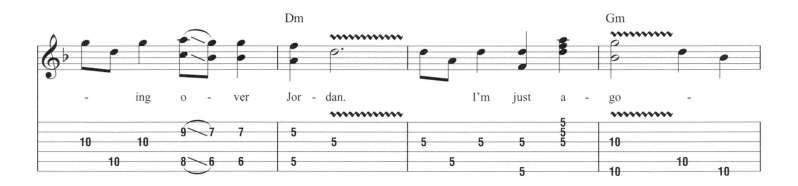

- ing o - ver Jor - dan. I'm just a go -

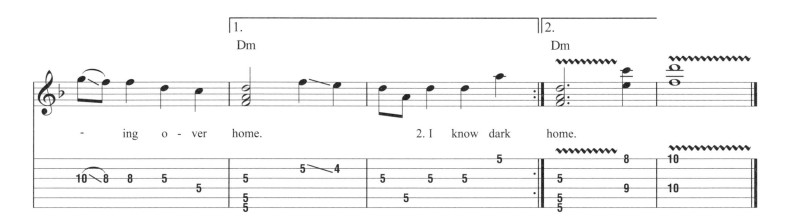

- ing o - ver home. 2. I know dark home.

Additional Lyrics

2. I know dark clouds will gather 'round me. I know my way is rough and steep.
But beautiful fields lie just beyond me, where souls redeemed their vigil keep.

Chorus I'm going there to meet my mother. She said she'd meet me when I come.
I'm just a-going over Jordan. I'm only going over home.

Wildwood Flower

Words and Music by A.P. Carter

One of the Carter Family's most often-covered songs, "Wildwood Flower" was inspired by one or possibly two nineteenth-century parlor songs.* It became Maybelle Carter's signature tune and for decades it was considered a rite of passage for an acoustic guitarist to learn how to pick the tune as an instrumental.

*Songs sung around the piano for entertainment in the living room (parlor)

G tuning:
(low to high) G-B-D-G-B-D

Key of C

Verse

Bright Two-Beat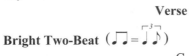

1. Oh, I'll twine with my min - gles and

2., 3. *See additional lyrics*

wav - ing black hair, with the

ros - es so red and the lil - ies so

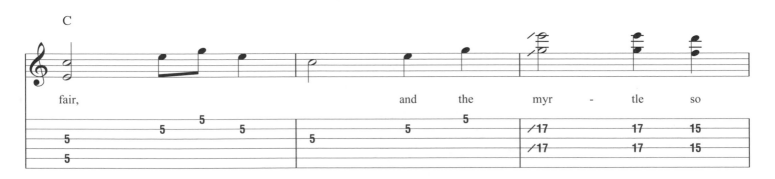

fair, and the myr - tle so

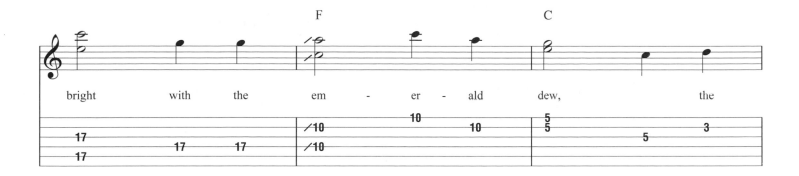

bright   with   the   em - er - ald   dew,   the

pale   and   the   lead - er   and   eyes   look   like

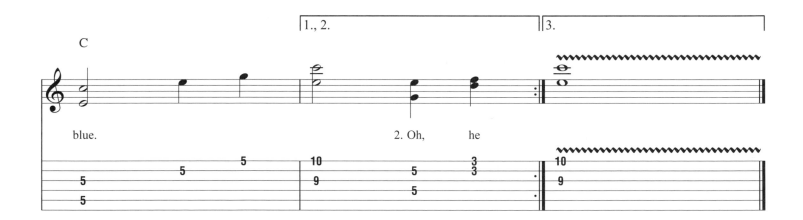

blue.   2. Oh,   he

Additional Lyrics

2. Oh, he taught me to love him and promised to love
    And to cherish me over all others above.
    How my heart is now wondering, no misery can tell.
    He's left me no warning, no words of farewell.

3. Oh, he taught me to love him and called me his flower,
    That was blooming to cheer him through life's dreary hour.
    Oh, I long to see him and regret the dark hour.
    He's gone and neglected this pale wildwood flower.

You Are My Sunshine

Words and Music by Jimmie Davis

One of the United States' most popular songs, "You Are My Sunshine" was made famous by country singer/governor of Louisiana, Jimmie Davis' 1940 recording. It has been covered by singers of all genres, including Bing Crosby, Ray Charles, Chuck Berry, The Beach Boys, Nat "King" Cole, Burl Ives, Gene Autry, Mississippi John Hurt, Mose Allison, and many more! Once again, this arrangement shows how to play the melody both up and down the fretboard. The lower-register version has three-finger rolls filling the pauses in the melody.

G tuning:
(low to high) G-B-D-G-B-D

Key of G

𝄋 **Chorus**

Moderate Country Shuffle

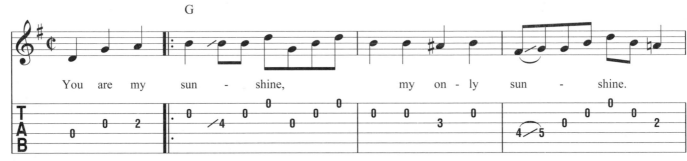

You are my sun - shine, my on - ly sun - shine.

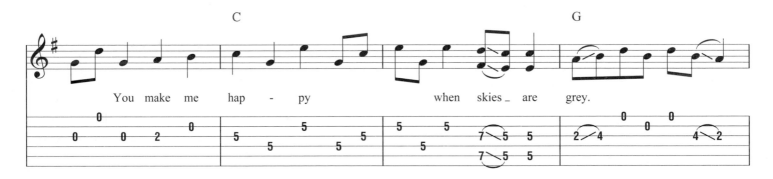

You make me hap - py when skies _ are grey.

You'll nev - er know, dear, how much I love you.

To Coda ⊕

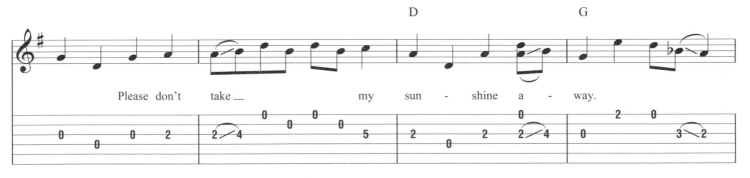

Please don't take _ my sun - shine a - way.

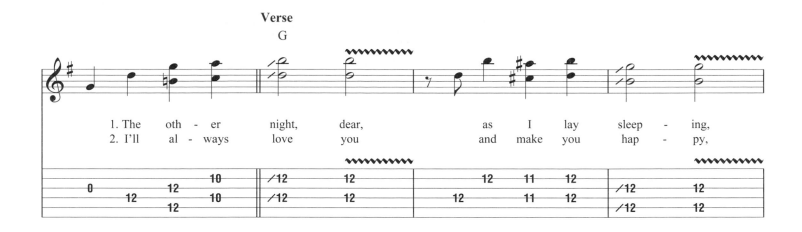

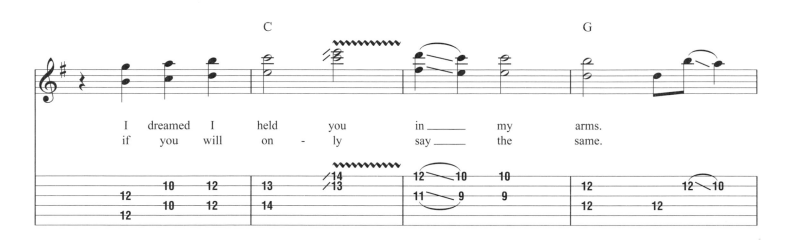

2nd time, D.S. al Coda ⊕ **Coda**

Your Cheatin' Heart

Words and Music by Hank Williams

Hank Williams' last recording session (in 1952) was attended by his fiancée, Billie Jean Jones, and his former girlfriend, Bobbie Jett (with an ex-boyfriend in tow). Bobbie Jett came uninvited to confront Hank—she was pregnant with his child. In this soap opera atmosphere, Williams recorded four songs, including "Your Cheatin' Heart." Probably written to his ex-wife Audrey, it became Hank's theme song after his death. He may have never performed this tune live, but it went to #1 on the charts and many vocalists have charted with it over the years.

C6 tuning:
(low to high) C-E-G-A-C-E

Key of C

GUITAR NOTATION LEGEND

Guitar music can be notated three different ways: on a *musical staff*, in *tablature*, and in *rhythm slashes*.

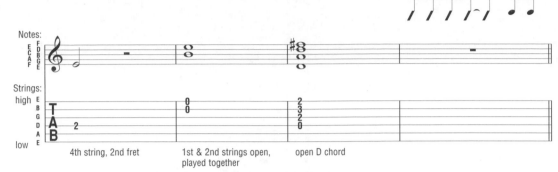

RHYTHM SLASHES are written above the staff. Strum chords in the rhythm indicated. Use the chord diagrams found at the top of the first page of the transcription for the appropriate chord voicings. Round noteheads indicate single notes.

THE MUSICAL STAFF shows pitches and rhythms and is divided by bar lines into measures. Pitches are named after the first seven letters of the alphabet.

TABLATURE graphically represents the guitar fingerboard. Each horizontal line represents a string, and each number represents a fret.

4th string, 2nd fret

1st & 2nd strings open, played together

open D chord

HALF-STEP BEND: Strike the note and bend up 1/2 step.

WHOLE-STEP BEND: Strike the note and bend up one step.

GRACE NOTE BEND: Strike the note and immediately bend up as indicated.

SLIGHT (MICROTONE) BEND: Strike the note and bend up 1/4 step.

BEND AND RELEASE: Strike the note and bend up as indicated, then release back to the original note. Only the first note is struck.

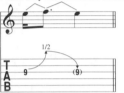

PRE-BEND: Bend the note as indicated, then strike it.

VIBRATO: The string is vibrated by rapidly bending and releasing the note with the fretting hand.

WIDE VIBRATO: The pitch is varied to a greater degree by vibrating with the fretting hand.

HAMMER-ON: Strike the first (lower) note with one finger, then sound the higher note (on the same string) with another finger by fretting it without picking.

PULL-OFF: Place both fingers on the notes to be sounded. Strike the first note and without picking, pull the finger off to sound the second (lower) note.

LEGATO SLIDE: Strike the first note and then slide the same fret-hand finger up or down to the second note. The second note is not struck.

SHIFT SLIDE: Same as legato slide, except the second note is struck.

TRILL: Very rapidly alternate between the notes indicated by continuously hammering on and pulling off.

TAPPING: Hammer ("tap") the fret indicated with the pick-hand index or middle finger and pull off to the note fretted by the fret hand.

NATURAL HARMONIC: Strike the note while the fret-hand lightly touches the string directly over the fret indicated.

Harm.

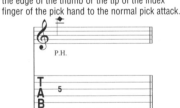

PINCH HARMONIC: The note is fretted normally and a harmonic is produced by adding the edge of the thumb or the tip of the index finger of the pick hand to the normal pick attack.

P.H.

PICK SCRAPE: The edge of the pick is rubbed down (or up) the string, producing a scratchy sound.

P.S.

MUFFLED STRINGS: A percussive sound is produced by laying the fret hand across the string(s) without depressing, and striking them with the pick hand.

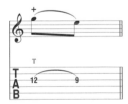

PALM MUTING: The note is partially muted by the pick hand lightly touching the string(s) just before the bridge.

P.M.

RAKE: Drag the pick across the strings indicated with a single motion.

rake

TREMOLO PICKING: The note is picked as rapidly and continuously as possible.

VIBRATO BAR DIVE AND RETURN: The pitch of the note or chord is dropped a specified number of steps (in rhythm), then returned to the original pitch.

w/ bar

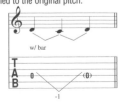

VIBRATO BAR SCOOP: Depress the bar just before striking the note, then quickly release the bar.

w/ bar

VIBRATO BAR DIP: Strike the note and then immediately drop a specified number of steps, then release back to the original pitch.

w/ bar